THE ASSE...

POPULAR
HISTORY

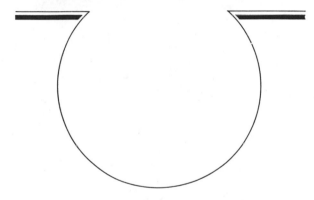

EDITH WALDVOGEL BLUMHOFER

RadiantBOOKS

Gospel Publishing House/Springfield, Mo. 65802

Printed in the United States of America

02-0469

Library of Congress Catalog Card Number 85-07552
International Standard Book Number 0-88243-469-1
Printed in the United States of America

Contents

Foreword

Dr. Edith L. Blumhofer of Springfield, Missouri, has already made her mark as a historian. A graduate of Hunter College (City University of New York) with an undergraduate degree in history and an M.A. in American history, she earned her Ph.D. at Harvard University majoring in American religion. She attended Harvard on a Danforth Fellowship.

Mrs. Blumhofer was born into a longtime Pentecostal family. Her parents and grandparents, the Waldvogels, are well known in the East and the Chicago-Milwaukee area, as well as in Germany. She has traveled in Europe and Canada. Her writings have been published in numerous magazines and journals.

Among the many qualifications she has to write *The Assemblies of God: A Popular History* is her deep commitment to our Lord and to Assemblies of God doctrine and practice.

This account of the Assemblies of God furnishes a concise, readable history of the largest American Pentecostal denomination.

The author takes the reader back beyond the formation of the Fellowship in 1914. She states, "Our story must begin earlier . . . for the . . . origins of the Assemblies of God are in the complex religious culture of the late 19th century."

Drawing from the political, social, and religious events following the Civil War, she skillfully sets forth the converging circumstances that laid the groundwork for the Pentecostal revival of this century. After sketching the background, she tells the dramatic story of the development of the Assemblies of God in the seven decades that followed.

The reader will sense the eternal purpose of God being fulfilled according to His sovereign time schedule. The "fulness of time was come" for God to manifest himself in this vibrant church body which He has used to touch millions throughout the world.

This short volume will contribute much to the historical record of a worldwide Fellowship of nearly 15 million adherents.

> G. RAYMOND CARLSON
> ASSISTANT GENERAL SUPERINTENDENT
> OF THE ASSEMBLIES OF GOD

Preface

American Pentecostalism finds many expressions. Its followers worship in storefront missions, wealthy congregations, small churches, home Bible studies, and religious communities. They come from all social classes and ethnic backgrounds. Some join Pentecostal denominations; some worship in old-line denominations. Some reject all denominations and cherish the congregational independence prized by leaders of the early 20th-century Pentecostal revival.

In this many-sided Movement, over 1 million American believers identify with the Assemblies of God. One of the early Pentecostal groups, the Assemblies of God is also among the fastest-growing major evangelical denominations. Its stability has made it a leader in both the American and international Pentecostal movements.

The Assemblies of God is people—people in all walks of life, with varying views of worship and life-style, united by their commitment to Jesus Christ and their understanding of the Holy Spirit's ministry. They share a rich heritage.

The following pages are an attempt to examine that heritage. All dates, names, and quotes are from firsthand sources of information. The emphasis throughout is on the American fellowship as a whole; space does not allow consideration of district and regional developments.

I owe special gratitude to the Board of Publication of the Assemblies of God for its authorization of this work and its assistance along the way. The interest and support of the administration of Evangel College and Dr. J. C. Holsinger, chairperson of Evangel's Social Sciences Department, also helped make this book possible.

The headquarters staff has been consistently helpful. I am especially indebted to Wayne Warner, director of the Assemblies of God Archives, and his assistant, Andre Rigden, who helped at every stage of the project. I am grateful to the editorial staff at Gospel Publishing House for clarifying and improving this manuscript.

My interest in the origins of Pentecostalism came much earlier than my doctoral work at Harvard University. It began at home, where my parents, Edwin and Edith Waldvogel, consistently lived the Pentecostal message Dad preached. They gave me an appreciation for the people and events described in this book. I am deeply grateful for my parents' example and encouragement and for the "goodly heritage" they have given me.

Like all my undertakings, this book would have been impossible without the understanding cooperation of my husband, Edwin. To him, and to our three children, I express appreciation for the patience and love that make ours a happy home.

1

The Evangelical Heritage

The Assemblies of God is an outgrowth of the world-wide Pentecostal revival that broke out in 1901. Its official history begins in Hot Springs, Arkansas, in April 1914. Our story must begin earlier, however, for the immediate origins of the Assemblies of God are in the complex religious culture of the late 19th century.

At the end of the Civil War, in 1865, Americans faced a new era. Disagreements over Reconstruction and civil rights created unprecedented political and social problems. Major Protestant denominations that had split before the war remained divided. The physical move from the farm to the city, from the field to the factory; the mental move from religious thinking to secular thinking, segregating God from the world at large—these changed values and life-styles. At the same time, the arrival of large numbers of Orientals, Catholics, and Jews represented a shift in immigration patterns.

Bible scholars, especially in British and German universities, questioned truths long regarded as fundamentals of the faith. American Protestant liberalism gained momentum.

Charles Darwin's books, *Origin of Species* (1859) and *Descent of Man* (1870), raised issues that would revolutionize science, divide denominations, and help shape the disciplines we know as the social sciences.

Some responded to these new situations by clearly recommitting themselves to both the verbal inspiration of Scripture and the evangelical faith. Their efforts helped form the fundamentalist component in American evangelicalism and contributed significantly to the Pentecostal heritage.

The Fundamentalist Component

During the late 19th century, Evangelist Dwight Lyman Moody preached to large crowds around the United States and throughout Britain. Of humble New England stock, Moody had left Boston for Chicago. There he began a ministry that eventually reached across the Atlantic. Although he lacked formal ministerial training, Moody strongly influenced the evangelical culture of his day. His commitment to evangelism motivated his tireless efforts to find ways to win the world to Christ.

During the 1870s, Moody came under the influence of the English Brethren movement (commonly known as Plymouth Brethren). The Brethren had their origins in British prophetic conferences where the subject of the end times was considered. Under the general leadership of John Nelson Darby and others, they taught that the Second Coming was rapidly approaching. They also developed a system of Biblical interpretation known as dispensationalism.

The Brethren convinced Moody that their teaching of Christ's imminent return was Biblical. This view contrasted sharply with American religious thinking of the day. In this country many hoped to Christianize society through political and social reform.

Moody and those American evangelicals who agreed that Christ's coming was near rejected such schemes. Instead they maintained: "In the return of Christ is the perfect solution—the only solution—to the problems of this age." They described Christ's return as "always imminent," and they regarded their acceptance of this viewpoint as a "second conversion." It clearly reordered their priorities. Reflecting on his own altered life-style, Moody said: "It was as if God had given me a lifeboat and said to me, 'Moody, save all you can.'"

Those evangelicals convinced of Christ's soon return found it motivated them in the area of evangelism. Since they believed they were living in the last days, their task was momentous: the evangelization of the world in their generation. For that, they clearly needed supernatural ability to proclaim Christ. As they studied Scripture for direction, they soon began to focus on the person and work of the Holy Spirit.

Their study of Scripture indicated that spiritual power was available to them in a special experience of baptism in the Holy Spirit. This baptism, they discovered, was "enduement with power for service." It made service obligatory. It gave power for "unwearied work," and they took its availability seriously. "If I *may* be baptized with the Spirit, I *must* be," wrote Moody's associate, Reuben Archer Torrey. His conclusions shattered religious complacency: "If I am not willing to pay the price of this baptism, and therefore am not so baptized, I am responsible before God for all the souls that might have been saved but were not saved through me because I was not baptized with the Holy Spirit."

Torrey urged his contemporaries to open their minds to "larger works" of God: "If we wish the mightiest possible work of God in our own souls," Torrey declared at the Northfield (Massachusetts) Conference in 1895, "when we read of any larger work of God in the Bible, or hear someone tell of it in his experience, let us not try to trim it down to our present poor experience, and save our pride. Let us throw our pride overboard, and humbly

11

confess, 'Here is something I do not possess,' and then get it."

This was one way in which Americans rediscovered the doctrine of Spirit baptism. Compelled by their premillennialism to win their world, they prayed for power to fulfill that task. This emphasis became especially meaningful to those involved in Moody's various ministries. By the 1890s they had begun to teach the necessity of a special "enduement with power for service."

In the light of an "any-moment" Second Coming, personal holiness was also urgent. So continuous communion with the person of the Holy Spirit was stressed by Moody, Torrey, and some of their fellow evangelicals (like Boston Baptist spokesman Adoniram Judson Gordon and New York City pastor Albert Benjamin Simpson).

They admitted that their focus on the Spirit as a Person differed significantly from what most Protestants were teaching. Generally speaking, they thought their colleagues tended to stress the Spirit as a power or an influence rather than as a Person. They regarded this as a serious inaccuracy. Because the Spirit was a Person "infinitely wise" and "infinitely tender," they maintained, He coveted fellowship. Carelessness and sin grieved Him. If permitted to do His work in the individual, however, He would overcome sin, make the believer aware of His constant presence, and accomplish, moment by moment, His sanctifying work.

A renewed awareness of Christ naturally followed this emphasis on the Holy Spirit. The Spirit revealed Christ. For A. B. Simpson, even the special "enduement with power for service" was Christ-centered. He expressed this concept in words that many early Pentecostals sang:

> Jesus only is our Power,
> His the gift of Pentecost.

Jesus, breathe Thy power upon us,
Fill us with the Holy Ghost.

The baptism in the Holy Spirit brought much more than "power to serve"; the Holy Spirit represented "power to be" as well. The believer was enabled to enter into a new dimension of worship and adoration. The vital relationship with Christ—this "reign of Christ within the soul"—was an essential part of the "walk in the Spirit." The Holy Spirit constantly drew the believer to Christ.

These emphases on power for service and walking in the Spirit, then, became, for an important group of late 19th-century evangelicals, logical outcomes of their expectation of Christ's soon coming. For the most part, premillennialist teaching found acceptance among people in denominations with roots in the Reformation ideas of followers of John Calvin: Baptists, Presbyterians, Congregationalists.

As they studied the Bible, some of those who stressed anew the ministry of the Holy Spirit—people like Torrey, Gordon, and Simpson—also concluded that Christ could meet earthly as well as spiritual needs. Many of these, at least for a time, practiced "faith" living: Accepting no regular salary, they prayed about all of their needs and recorded their answers to prayer.

In such ventures, George Mueller, a British Brethren leader who had founded large faith orphanages in Bristol, England, deeply influenced Americans. Mueller cared for hundreds of orphans without visible means of support. His reports circulated widely in America, and during several tours of the United States, his godliness and humility won him deep respect. His stories of miraculous provision inspired some to imitate him.

As Biblical literalists, these evangelicals also concluded that divine healing was in the Atonement. (In this,

Moody's associates differed with Moody, who never preached physical healing.) Once they had concluded that they lived in the last days, some had come to expect a "latter rain" revival. "As these signs marked the period of [Christ's] presence on earth," said A. B. Simpson, "so they will attend His return." This concept of "full salvation" (that is, salvation for spirit, soul, and body) was rooted, then, in their conviction that they were in the last days.

D. L. Moody provided some important social structures in which the new stress on the Holy Spirit was presented. Annual conferences at Northfield, Massachusetts, became retreats in which American and British leaders developed the themes of the Spirit's endowment and the individual's walk in the Spirit. Also at Northfield gospel songs were widely used to help popularize the themes. "Moment by Moment I'm Kept in His Love," by Moody's friend Major D. W. Whittle, described the experience of the indwelling Christ and communion with the Spirit. "The Comforter Has Come" (with its assertion: "The long, long night is past; the morning breaks at last") captured the general conviction that a new move of the Spirit was under way.

Moody's Northfield Conferences also had a strong missions emphasis. The eminent Arthur T. Pierson, editor of *The Missionary Review of the World*, directed the missions program. At Northfield, the Student Volunteer Movement, which mobilized thousands of America's youth for missions, was born. Under its slogan—"the evangelization of the world in this generation"—it became part of the great missions thrust of the late 19th century.

During the 1890s, Moody invited speakers from the annual British Keswick Conventions to Northfield to teach on the Spirit-filled life. In this way, American evangelicals were personally introduced to the ministries of people like F. B. Meyer, Andrew Murray, and Evan Hopkins.

Actually, Keswick teaching had been developed in the early 1870s by two American evangelists, R. Pearsall Smith and William E. Boardman. But it was Smith's wife, Hannah, who gave their thought classic statement with her *Christian's Secret of a Happy Life.* Keswick teaching said that most Christians were "grievously destitute of real spiritual power and often essentially carnal." Nonetheless, it was "the duty and privilege of every child of God at once to enter into newness of life, and walk henceforth in the power of Christ's resurrection." To accomplish this, Keswick spokespersons challenged believers to experience inner changes that would culminate in "enducment with power and infilling with the Holy Spirit."

As Keswick teaching became known in America it popularized (as it had in Britain) concepts and language that the Pentecostal movement would use in the next century. It was claimed that Moody's introduction of Keswick emphases at Northfield was part of an effort to balance the practical stress of American Christians. They emphasized Spirit baptism as "power for service," while the British taught an experiential piety, "the reign of Christ within the soul."

Another of the structures Moody used that would have lasting influence on both fundamentalism and Pentecostalism was the Bible institute. What Moody observed convinced him that seminaries educated ministers away from the urban masses. In response, he developed a practical training program.

His Chicago Training Institute (now Moody Bible Institute) had as its goal the training of men and women to stand in the gap between the educated clergy and the common people. The school offered courses in the English Bible (not the original Greek and Hebrew), in gospel music, and in basic English, and then sent its students out to spend part of each regular school day in ministry on the streets of Chicago. A high school diploma was not required for admission, and the school, with R. A. Torrey as its first superintendent, quickly attracted hundreds of students.

Canadian-born A. B. Simpson directed another ministry that popularized similar themes and methods. Simpson left the pastorate of a well-to-do Presbyterian congregation in New York City to begin an independent outreach in that city. It soon included healing homes, an inner-city congregation, a Bible institute, and a strong missions emphasis.

Simpson also conducted regular conferences at the campground at Old Orchard Beach, Maine. They drew hundreds from many denominations who shared Simpson's commitment to a fourfold gospel of Christ: the Saviour, Sanctifier, Healer, and soon-coming King. His various ministries expanded until he gave them loose organizational structure as the Christian and Missionary Alliance.

The Restorationist Drive

Because these evangelicals emphasized that they were in the last days, they often spoke of a "latter rain" outpouring that would mark the time of Christ's return. This latter-day revival would restore not only the spiritual gifts but New Testament Christianity as well. But some took this restorationist thinking to an extreme degree—John Alexander Dowie, for example. But in stimulating interest in the restoration of apostolic Christianity, he made an important contribution to the Pentecostal heritage.

A Scotsman by birth and education, Dowie spent his childhood in Australia. He pastored Congregational churches there until he came to the United States in 1888. During the 1893 Chicago World's Fair, he set up his ministry in Chicago. Noted for his success in praying for the sick, Dowie claimed to possess a gift of healing. Outspoken and controversial, he denounced the medical profession and all drugs, as well as all other teachers of divine healing who permitted their use. He gathered around him in a relatively short time an international following estimated at over 20,000.

Dowie's theme of healing in the Atonement was relatively new in America; it had been proclaimed popularly for barely a generation. Baptist pastor A. J. Gordon had written the most important contemporary book on the subject, *The Ministry of Healing*, in 1882.

The subject gained support in evangelical ranks at the same time that Mary Baker Eddy introduced her Christian Science teaching. In part, such support was a response to Christian Science and other unorthodox healing efforts. In addition, the introduction of healing was closely related to both the expectation of an end-times renewal and the concept of a full salvation. In the United States by the 1890s, there were at least 30 faith homes, most of which ministered to the sick by offering lodging and instruction as well as prayer. Dowie's outspoken manner simply made him the most conspicuous and controversial among a growing group who believed that healing was in the Atonement.

In time, Dowie organized his followers into a new denomination, the Christian Catholic Church. In 1900 he unveiled plans for a Christian community void of doctors, drugs, tobacco, liquor, or pork products. More than 6,000 responded to his invitation to live in the community, which would become Zion, Illinois.

Increasingly intrigued with restorationist themes, Dowie declared himself Elijah the Restorer in 1901. In

1904, he proclaimed himself an apostle and changed the name of his organization to Christian Catholic Apostolic Church. He expected an orderly restoration of all the New Testament gifts and the revelation of 11 other apostles. Before that occurred, he was deposed, the victim of his own financial mismanagement and novel interpretation of Scripture. With his removal from office, the apostolic restorationist idea disappeared from his church. By that time, however, his Zion had nurtured many who would soon see in Pentecostalism the fulfillment of Dowie's dream of restoration.

Dowie was but one among several having similar dreams. Frank Sandford of Shiloh, Maine, also claimed to be Elijah the Restorer. Ambrose Jessup Tomlinson, a Bible society salesman, traveled up and down the east coast in an effort to find any who had experienced "the primitive faith." In 1903, he would claim that God had restored through him the (exclusive) Church of God.

In many places, however, restorationist expectations took a more traditional form. Small groups of earnest Christians severed their ties to denominations and formed Christian bands, or unions. Their goal was to express the simplicity of the apostolic faith and to experience its reality for themselves.

The Wesleyan Contribution

The Wesleyan tradition also prepared many who longed to experience piety. John Wesley's doctrine of Christian perfection said a believer could be freed from the desire to sin through an experience of perfect love. Americans modified Wesley's original concept that had allowed for both gradual and instantaneous perfection and taught that the experience should always be instantaneous. The claim that a "second definite work of grace" should always be the norm was identified in late 19th-century America with the holiness movements.

Before the Civil War, among Methodists and others, the teaching had flourished, promoted by such publications as *The Guide to Holiness* and by such itinerant ministries as that of Walter and Phoebe Palmer. In those years it had had important social consequences: It poured vitality into the reform efforts of individuals wanting to perfect their society as well as their souls.

After the war, the desire for piety had again become a crusade. It was spearheaded by those leaders of the Methodist Episcopal Church, North, who gathered in Vineland, New Jersey, in 1867 to create the National Camp Meeting Association for the Promotion of Holiness. Holiness camp meetings became the settings in which thousands from all denominations professed a second religious crisis experience. They referred to it by many names: sanctification, perfect love, Christian perfection, second blessing, baptism with the Holy Spirit, to cite a few. Whatever it was called, it suggested a moment of consecration and cleansing. For some, it included a concept of being endowed with power.

To some Methodist leaders, however, holiness teaching symbolized a growing exclusivism. In 1894, the Methodist Episcopal Church, South, objected to the tendency of those identified with the holiness movement to imply that they had a monopoly on the experience of holiness. "They have changed the name of our meetings, substituting Holiness for Methodist," reported the *Wesleyan Advocate*. The *Journal* of the Methodist Episcopal Church, South, criticized their separatism: "They have holiness associations, holiness meetings, holiness preachers, holiness evangelists, and holiness property. . . . We deplore their teaching and methods in so far as they claim a monopoly of the experience, practice, and advocacy of holiness, and separate themselves from the body of ministers and disciples."

By the 1890s Methodist leadership, both North and South, urged members to affirm their loyalty by bringing their quest for holiness under the supervision of the denomination. The vast majority of Methodists obeyed. Others, however, refused and formed local holiness missions and associations. Some of these groups were short-lived. But others expanded by amalgamation and evangelism to become denominations. (The largest of these would become the Church of the Nazarene.) Advocacy of the "second blessing" and a stress on holy living, or separation from the world, characterized such independent holiness groups.

By the turn of the century, then, in various settings in the American religious culture, a renewed emphasis on the Holy Spirit had become apparent. Other doctrines of "apostolic" Christianity were also being proclaimed. Early in the new century came an event that tended to intensify spiritual desire: Americans began to hear of a remarkable revival in Wales.

The Welsh Revival

The Welsh Revival had neither leader nor programs, yet "swept the country with the order of an attacking force." It revolutionized spiritual life in Wales in 1904 and 1905. Its challenge became "bend the church, and save the world." Evan Roberts, a converted miner, gave the revival a degree of unity by his itinerant ministry.

From the beginning of the Welsh Revival, participants claimed it was only the foretaste of a worldwide renewal. "Wonderful things have happened in Wales . . . but these are only a beginning," wrote Roberts. "The world will be swept by His Spirit as by a rushing, mighty wind. . . .

Thousands upon thousands will do more than we have accomplished, as God gives them power." Roberts explicitly linked the revival with the fulfillment of Joel's prophecy as quoted in Acts 2: "And it shall come to pass in the last days, saith God, I will pour out of my Spirit upon all flesh." From this point of view the revival had both end-time and Pentecostal meaning.

The language of the Welsh Revival would become part of Pentecostal terminology. The revival further popularized terms relating to spiritual power and matched them with specific types of experience. Participants described the meetings as having "Pentecostal character." The question put to the Ephesians by Paul—"Have ye received the Holy Ghost since ye believed?"—became "a question loudly ringing out to the Church of God through the Awakening in Wales," according to Jessie Penn-Lewis, one who was there.

Such language had been used in holiness ranks for some time. The Welsh Revival gave it renewed force just as Pentecostalism emerged. In the spontaneity and emotional fervor of Pentecostalism, some would readily see a continuation of the Welsh event.

Evangelicals (and curious spectators) from other countries arrived in Wales to report on the meetings. According to respected British evangelical G. Campbell Morgan, the services were "utterly without order, characterized from the first to the last by the orderliness of the Spirit of God." Evangelism was the product rather than the source of the renewal. Throughout Wales, spontaneous worship, testimonies, and prayer marked prolonged meetings, as crowds gathered with the simple desire to "see what the Holy Spirit would do."

Among its lessons, Morgan believed, were some addressing the Christian tendency to rely on organization and method. "It is divine visitation," Morgan concluded, "in which God . . . is saying to us: 'See what I can do without the things you are depending on; see what I can do in answer to a praying people; see what I can do through the simplest who are ready to fall in line and depend wholly and absolutely on me.' "

Visitors to Wales included some Americans. Many more Americans eagerly read the reports from the scene. Across the United States among holiness followers, and wherever Christ's soon return was expected, the records indicate renewed anticipation of an end-times revival. This latter rain would both equip the church to evangelize and prepare people to receive the message.

News from Wales encouraged Americans to believe the revival had begun and to expect a similarly powerful answer to their prayers. "When that remarkable revival broke out in Wales," wrote Elizabeth Baker (cofounder of the Elim ministry in Rochester, New York), "our hearts, like those of all Christendom, were greatly stirred. The Spirit of God moving so mightily, the absence of all human machinery, the tremendous results in the salvation of souls, made us very hungry to know God in His fullness."

Unknown to most of these evangelicals was the fact that only a few years earlier, in 1901, a ministry had begun in Kansas that would soon be proclaiming across the nation the full restoration of the "apostolic faith." The stage had been set by a generation of interdenominational teaching on the Holy Spirit and Christ's soon return and by the religious excitement from the Welsh Revival. Now the Pentecostal movement would challenge and, ultimately, divide those who in the late 19th century had yearned for an outpouring of the Holy Spirit.

2

The Rise of Pentecostalism

Pentecostalism has a rich 19th-century evangelical heritage. Wesleyans, restorationists, and others contributed to its vitality. But its first push came from a restorationist situation that had been deeply influenced by radical holiness thinking.

The Apostolic Faith

Among the many Americans concerned about holiness and spiritual power at the turn of the century was Charles Fox Parham. Born in Iowa in 1873, Parham spent much of his life in eastern Kansas, where he began preaching in 1889. Parham taught that holiness was a second definite work of grace and divine healing was in the Atonement. He gained a local reputation for success in healing ministry. More an itinerant evangelist than a pastor, he was largely self-educated in theology. At the beginning of his ministry he chose to be free from any religious affiliation and set out to experience the "apostolic faith."

In 1898, Parham and his wife, Sarah, opened a healing home in Topeka (a city with a population of just over 33,000). They also conducted nondenominational services with "mission doors ever open to all who preached the Gospel." "Our hearts," Parham wrote, "were stirred to deepen our consecration and to 'search the Word.' "

Like most of Parham's other enterprises, the healing home and mission were short-lived. Parham's "searching the Word" inspired him to travel to discover what others taught about the Holy Spirit. His visits to several important ministries (among them, Dowie's Zion and Simpson's Christian and Missionary Alliance) left him dissatisfied.

In the summer of 1900, Parham and several of his followers accepted an invitation to spend some time in Frank Sandford's community in Shiloh, Maine. The Topeka press reported that Parham meant to set up a similar work in Topeka.

Frank Sandford is one of the neglected figures in the involved story of Pentecostal origins around the turn of the century. Originally a Freewill Baptist, he objected to authority to such a degree that he launched his own independent faith ministry. A restorationist at heart, he declared himself Elijah the Restorer and preached a message of healing. By 1900 he had founded a community near Brunswick, Maine, which he called Shiloh, and opened a Bible school named The Holy Ghost and Us. Parham and his friends spent about 6 weeks at this center.

Sandford's Bible school clearly impressed Parham. It had one text, the Bible; one teacher, the Holy Spirit (speaking, of course, through Sandford); and a philosophy of education that encouraged "stopping whenever a truth was encountered which had not yet been experienced, and praying until it became part of our lives." Like many others in their day, Sandford's followers emphasized the Holy Spirit and referred to an experience of Spirit baptism.

In the fall of 1900 Parham returned to Topeka and opened a similar Bible school. About 40 students enrolled. Like Sandford, Parham had a practical purpose:

"Not to learn these things in our heads only, but have each thing in the Scriptures wrought out in our hearts . . . that every command that Jesus Christ gave should be literally obeyed."

The school was a classic example of the independent faith ministries of the day: "No one paid board or tuition; the poor were fed; the sick were entertained and healed; and from day to day, week to week, and month to month, with no sect or mission or known source of income back of us, God supplied our every need." The students studied together (with Parham as the only teacher and the Bible as the only text), assembled often for worship and prayer, and engaged in evangelism throughout the city.

By December, Parham's long fascination with the doctrine of the Holy Spirit resulted in an assignment for his students: to discover Biblical evidence for the baptism in the Holy Spirit. His peers who referred to such baptism generally associated it with either a purifying or empowering work of the Spirit. None had proposed a *uniform* initial evidence.

On the contrary, various radical views on evidence were put forth (such as the suggestion that certain physical behavior indicated Baptism); such views tended to discredit the doctrine. Respected evangelicals like R. A. Torrey, on the other hand, while agreeing that tongues *might* be evidence of Baptism, refused to specify a uniform evidence. They taught (as had Moody) that Spirit baptism would be shown by a desire "to learn more about Christ; a love for the Bible and a desire for spiritual knowledge and experience; disinterested love." "You shouldn't be looking for any token," Moody had advised. "Just keep asking and waiting for power."

Parham disagreed. And the lack of agreement on the matter of evidence of Spirit baptism troubled him. He regarded this as a hindrance to the effective proclamation of the experience.

Parham had already led his students through studies of the doctrines that would become the foundational truths of Pentecostalism: conversion, sanctification, healing, the premillennial return of Christ. (These were, of course, taught widely in the religious culture of which he was part.) Students were receptive: "As we spent much time in the presence of God," wrote Agnes Ozman, "He caused our hearts to be opened to all that is written."

Unlike the majority of those in the holiness movements, Parham had already separated the second definite work of grace from the baptism in the Holy Spirit. Rather than stressing two crisis experiences, he was moving in the direction of teaching three definite stages: conversion, sanctification, and Spirit baptism.

After completing their assignment, Parham's students agreed that the baptism in the Holy Spirit clothed the believer with power for service. They also agreed that the Biblical evidence of such baptism was always speaking in tongues. With this, a distinct Pentecostal movement was created within the ranks of those in the religious culture who had accepted—to this point—the essentials of Parham's teaching. Parham would maintain that the proclamation of the doctrine of Spirit baptism evidenced by tongues meant the apostolic faith had been fully recovered.

From the time of the students' watchnight service that ushered in 1901, people affiliated with Parham's ministry began to speak in tongues and to identify those tongues as evidence of their Spirit baptism. A few dissenters left the school, which soon disbanded in an effort to spread the apostolic faith.

For 2 years Parham struggled to maintain a Pentecostal ministry. But people seemed more interested in his belief that the British and American peoples were a part of the 10 "lost" tribes of Israel. His teaching on the Holy Spirit—and the future of the apostolic faith—appeared dim. Then in 1903, as the result of a remarkable healing in Eldorado Springs, Missouri, of Mary Arthur of Galena, Kansas, Parham was invited to Galena. The community flocked to the meetings to hear the man whose prayers had brought healing to their neighbor.

The Galena revival that followed became the turning point in Parham's ministry. He conducted meetings for months, first in a tent and then, as cool weather set in, in a warehouse seating 2,000. The meetings received coverage in the Kansas City and Topeka papers. Hundreds were saved, healed, and Spirit-filled. In Galena, the apostolic faith movement won young, dedicated evangelists who broadened its influence.

After the Galena revival, Parham and his apostolic faith bands, composed primarily of enthusiastic young converts, traveled widely in western Missouri and eastern Kansas as well as Oklahoma and Texas. They often announced their presence in town with a parade down the main street. Carrying banners reading "Apostolic Faith Movement," they sang songs and led the curious to their rented storefront mission or street meeting.

One participant reported the daily schedule: "We held two or three street meetings on different corners every night and visited from house to house during the mornings, by twos, stopping to pray if the people would let us, and we would tell them about the meetings. In the afternoon we would rest and pray for the meetings." In this way, they founded the faith missions that became the nucleus of the emerging Pentecostal movement.

In 1905, Parham set up a short-term Bible school in Houston, Texas, "supported, as was the rest of the work of the movement, by free-will offerings." He reported that "students did not have time for any study but the Bible." The teaching covered the subjects of conviction, repentance, conversion, consecration, sanctification, healing, the Holy Spirit, prophecies, and revelation. Among the students was a black Baptist holiness preacher, William J. Seymour. In the spring of the next year he would travel from Houston to Los Angeles.

The Los Angeles Revival

At the turn of the century, Los Angeles was a rapidly growing metropolis: Its population of 104,266 in 1900 more than tripled by 1910. In the city, a strong nucleus of Christians challenged by the Welsh Revival met regularly to pray for an evangelical awakening. Interdenominational Bible studies and prayer groups united those of all social classes who yearned for an outpouring of the Holy Spirit.

Besides these informal gatherings, a congregation of several hundred had formed the New Testament Church. Pastored by Joseph Smale, who had visited the Welsh Revival, this church sought to bring about a similar revival in Los Angeles. Its members prayed regularly for a full restoration of New Testament Christianity as part of a "latter-day" outpouring of the Holy Spirit.

Some of these people were inclined at least to consider the message Seymour would bring. In a short time, they found one another. Seymour's teaching on evidential tongues (which he had not yet experienced) got him ousted from the black holiness mission that had originally invited him. He moved his meetings: first to a private home (where he received his own Spirit baptism) and then to a large vacant building on Azusa Street. Services there continued day and night.

"Breathing strange utterances and mouthing a creed

which it would seem no sane mortal could understand, the newest religious sect has started in Los Angeles," reported the Wednesday, April 18, edition of the *Los Angeles Times*. "Meetings are held in a tumble-down shack on Azusa Street, and the devotees of the weird doctrines practice the most fanatical rites, preach the wildest theories, and work themselves into a state of mad excitement in their peculiar zeal."

Such "free advertising," participant Frank Bartleman recalled, "brought the crowds."

Among the crowds were hecklers and the curious as well as earnest seekers. When they arrived at Azusa Street, they found a continuous meeting. "Seeking souls could be found under the power almost any hour, night and day. . . . In that old building, with its low rafters and bare floors, God took strong men and women to pieces, and put them together again for His glory. It was a tremendous overhauling process," Bartleman reminisced.

Spontancity and expectancy marked each day's activities: "No subjects or sermons were announced ahead of time, and no special speakers for such an hour. No one knew what might be coming, what God would do. All was spontaneous, ordered of the Spirit." With time, however, in the spontaneity there did develop doctrinal and behavioral standards.

The apostolic faith, as Seymour proclaimed it in Los Angeles, set forth three stages in the salvation process. Believers were to be converted, sanctified, and Spirit-filled. These necessarily followed in sequence: a valid Spirit baptism came only on "the clean, sanctified life." Therefore, seekers were instructed first to be sanctified and then to be Spirit-filled. "Too many have confused the grace of sanctification with the enduement of power, or the baptism of the Holy Ghost," wrote Seymour. "The baptism of the Holy Ghost is a gift of power upon the sanctified life; so when we get it we have the same evidence as the disciples received on the day of Pentecost in speaking in new tongues."

Three themes became noticeable in the Azusa Street revival: (1) cleansing through the blood of Jesus, (2) the soon return of Christ, and (3) restorationism, or "unity" (which was, at the same time, a rejection of denominationalism).

Teaching on cleansing included an emphasis on confession and restitution. "The blood of Jesus will never blot out any sin between man and man they can make right," said Seymour. "But if we can't make wrongs right the blood graciously covers." As individuals "tarried" for their baptism, they were often reminded of past wrongs that needed to be made right. They repaid debts, apologized for old offenses, and made restitution for things stolen. They understood these actions to be necessary before being baptized in the Holy Spirit.

"The Apostolic Faith Movement," Seymour said, "stands for the restoration of the faith once delivered unto the saints—the old-time religion." Speaking in tongues was but one small part of the apostolic faith. Participants would later recall that there was a stronger emphasis on both the blood of Jesus and the Second Coming than on any spiritual gift (including tongues). The songs "There Is Power in the Blood" and "Under the Blood" were sung often, as was the joyous declaration "The Comforter Has Come."

Spontaneous worship marked the services. The experience of the Holy Spirit resulted in the exaltation of Christ. Participants in the Pentecostal revival were urged not to stress the baptism in the Holy Spirit as an end in itself. "Do you preach the baptism with the Holy Spirit?"

they were challenged, or "Do you preach Christ in the power of the baptism?"

Like other restorationists, early Pentecostals sincerely hoped to promote nondenominational fellowship rather than to create new denominations. Strongly congregationalist and antidenominational even before the denominations began to reject them, Pentecostals had tended to criticize if not to reject denominationalism in their pre-Pentecostal days. "We are not fighting men or churches," they insisted, "but seeking to displace dead forms and creeds of wild fanaticisms with living, practical Christianity. 'Love, Faith, Unity' is our watchword, and 'Victory Through the Atoning Blood' our battle cry."

As reports of continuing revival at Azusa Street spread around the country and to foreign missions stations, seekers began to come from many places. And some of them returned to their homes as evangelists of the new movement.

Proliferation and Problems

G. B. Cashwell brought Pentecostal teaching to small independent holiness groups in the south. As a result, the Pentecostal Holiness Church consolidated as a *tongues-speaking* Pentecostal ministry (the term *Pentecostal* was used by numerous non-tongues-speaking groups as well, creating some confusion). A. J. Tomlinson's Church of God also became Pentecostal. In Alabama, Cashwell won to the movement two former Methodist ministers, H. G. Rodgers and M. M. Pinson. These men would later bring some southern Pentecostals into the Assemblies of God. Many areas, primarily in the south, heard the Pentecostal message as a result of Cashwell's efforts. In some cases, organized groups joined the Pentecostal movement by adding to their statements of faith the Pentecostal distinctive on tongues.

In other cases, independent missions or local fellowships were formed.

Charles H. Mason—cofounder (with Charles Price Jones, author of many gospel songs popular with early Pentecostals) of the Church of God in Christ—received his baptism at Azusa Street. He then returned to Memphis to lead the majority of that group into the Pentecostal movement.

Parham, meanwhile, had accepted an invitation to Zion, Illinois, where Dowie's leadership had been repudiated and the city was in disarray. In a few weeks, and with considerable opposition, he set up a Pentecostal center in that city. During the winter of 1906/1907, he won to the movement gifted men and women who made a vital contribution to the Pentecostal revival, especially to the Assemblies of God. (His travels to Zion's missions in Canada and on the east coast were also important to the spread of Pentecostalism.)

Nearby Chicago, too, became an early Pentecostal center. William Hamner Piper, former overseer in Zion, had organized an independent evangelical congregation, the Stone Church, in Chicago. As a result of the Zion City revival, Piper brought his church into the Pentecostal movement. Chicago was home for several independent Pentecostal ministries—like the North Avenue Mission pastored by former Baptist William Durham—which played an important role in the early history of the Assemblies of God.

As the message preached by enthusiastic itinerant Pentecostal evangelists won followers, it also began to raise controversy. Among the groups most seriously challenged by the message was the Christian and Missionary Alliance.

In a revival at Simpson's Missionary Training Institute in 1907, several of the Alliance's young, promising leaders accepted Pentecostal teaching. In a matter of months, entire Alliance congregations became Pentecostal. After a period of uncertainty in responding to Pentecostalism, Alliance leaders virtually excluded tongues-speaking from their movement: They adopted the position that tongues should neither be sought nor forbidden. Alliance spokesmen believed that *any* gift might evidence Spirit baptism. In this way they rejected both the Pentecostal focus on tongues as the evidence of the Baptism and the Pentecostal distinction between tongues as *evidence* and tongues as a *gift*.

Nevertheless, the heritage that a strong nucleus of followers brought from the Christian and Missionary Alliance greatly enriched the Assemblies of God. Alliance founder A. B. Simpson was a man of faith, dedicated to evangelism, and convinced of the reality of New Testament Christianity in his day. He imparted his vision to a number of men and women who became Assemblies of God leaders.

The great majority of Pentecostals did not belong to centralized fellowships. Rather they worshiped in independent missions and churches across the country. This resistance to a centralized authority was a matter of belief almost as much as the gospel, for many vowed never to revert to "dead" denominational forms. Before the Pentecostal movement had survived a decade, however, problems threatened its future. By 1913 the more thoughtful believers recognized that some organization of the independent elements could both guard the movement from error and aid its growth.

The difficulties that beset the movement had both outside and inside origins. Exaggerated reports of fanaticism gave rise to false stereotypes. As Editor J. R. Flower wrote, "There is a so-called 'free Pentecost' in this country, and one can find almost any practice in the 'free' Pentecostal assemblies."

Some evangelicals reacted strongly against Pentecostal assertions that those who had not spoken in tongues had never received Spirit baptism. Occasionally, Pentecostals claimed to be more spiritual than those who disagreed with them on the matter of initial evidence. For a variety of reasons, many Pentecostals found it impossible to remain in the churches where they had fellowshipped earlier. Everywhere, the Pentecostal message aroused controversy.

"The devil is raging, the saints are shouting, and God is working," wrote Editor Eudorus N. Bell. Some Pentecostals felt threatened by the "raging," while others were confident that the "shouting" was victorious.

Itinerant, noncredentialed evangelists sometimes proved they did not merit the confidence of believers; Pentecostal periodicals issued warnings against them by name. Occasionally missionaries left for foreign countries without enough support, sometimes with no intention of studying the language of their field (convinced they could communicate through tongues). In a few cases, their "call" was based on the language someone had told them they had spoken at the moment of their Spirit baptism.

In the United States, short-term Bible schools occasionally relied on prophecy and tongues and interpretation for instruction, and used these gifts for personal direction (whom to marry, for example). The mission at Azusa Street, meanwhile, had allowed some practices that other Pentecostals rejected and had become largely a black outreach.

Parham's leadership was rejected by his most capable associates because of persistent charges of sexual wrongdoing. Doctrinal issues had also been raised; the movement was badly fragmented and in desperate need of a standard of conduct and doctrine.

The Hot Springs General Council

The call for order came from southern Pentecostals led by E. N. Bell. After his Spirit baptism he had found a warm welcome among a group of young, enthusiastic Pentecostal preachers in Texas who had recently renounced Charles Parham's leadership. They continued to call their movement the Apostolic Faith, but were fully independent from established groups using that name. Bell was older, more experienced, and better educated than most of them and soon became a recognized leader. He assumed the editorial responsibilities of their paper, the *Apostolic Faith*.

Gradually, Bell and his associates began to favor the term *Pentecostal* over *Apostolic Faith*. The group came into fellowship with H. G. Rodgers and other independent Pentecostals in the southeast to form a loosely knit organization: The Church of God in Christ and in unity with the Apostolic Faith Movement. By 1913, its ministerial list included 352 names and the group's name had been shortened to the Church of God in Christ. An informal relationship was maintained with the holiness Pentecostal group of the same name.

At a camp meeting in Eureka Springs, Arkansas, Bell decided to merge his *Apostolic Faith* with the *Word and Witness*, edited by M. M. Pinson. Bell kept the title *Word and Witness* and began to publish the paper from his home base in Malvern, Arkansas.

The Church of God in Christ was simply a loose ministerial association without binding authority—a "gentlemen's agreement," participants called it. Some believed more organization was needed to prevent cliques from

35

"galloping off each in its own direction," so Bell and others called a General Council to convene at Hot Springs in April 1914. An invitation was extended through Pentecostal papers to "the saints everywhere."

Word and Witness listed five general purposes for the Hot Springs meeting: unity ("that we may do away with so many divisions, both in doctrines and in the various names under which our Pentecostal people are working and incorporating"); stabilization ("conserving the work, that we may all build up and not tear down"); effective missions outreach; legal chartering of the movement; and the consideration of a Bible school to serve Pentecostals.

Given the antidenominational bias of the apostolic faith and holiness movements, the call to Hot Springs aroused considerable internal opposition. By 1914, conservative evangelical leaders had begun to attack Pentecostalism. This reinforced the Pentecostals' positions rejecting denominationalism and creedal statements. They feared what any move toward centralized authority might mean.

Nonetheless, over 300 arrived in Hot Springs, 128 registering as ministers and missionaries. Among them were representatives of at least five centers of Pentecostal ministry that would influence the early development of the Assemblies of God: (1) the Christian and Missionary Alliance, (2) Dowie's Zion, (3) Chicago's various missions, (4) Parham's Apostolic Faith work in Texas and Arkansas, and (5) the Alabama-based Church of God in Christ.

They came with the opinion that the advantages of "cooperative fellowship" and general standards for conduct and practice far outweighed any disadvantages. In recent issues of the *Word and Witness*, Bell had developed the argument in favor of organization: Not only would it eliminate abuses, it would also promote efficiency. The anticipated results of organization included expansion of publishing capabilities, coordination of missionary efforts, and the promotion of education.

The convention opened on Thursday, April 2, for 4 days of emphasis on prayer and fellowship. Business sessions began on Monday, April 6, under the supervision of E. N. Bell as temporary chairman and J. Roswell Flower, evangelist and editor of the *Christian Evangel*, as secretary.

Several days of careful, prayerful work resulted in the formation of the Assemblies of God. Rejecting denominational organization, delegates agreed to promote a voluntary cooperation that would not affect congregational self-government. They decided that local assemblies would be referred to by "the general scriptural name, 'Assembly of God.'" Representatives of local congregations would make up the General Council of the Assemblies of God, the purpose of which was "to recognize Scriptural methods and order for worship, unity, fellowship, work and business for God and to disapprove of all unscriptural methods, doctrine and conduct." Delegates voted to incorporate under the name "General Council of the Assemblies of God."

The Hot Springs General Council did not adopt a statement of faith. Delegates simply agreed that the Bible was "the all-sufficient rule for faith and practice." They named E. N. Bell and J. R. Flower to remain as general chairman and secretary-treasurer until the next convention. They also set up a 12-member Executive Presbytery to serve a 1-year term and selected Bell's *Word and Witness* as the official organ of the Fellowship. (Flower's *Christian Evangel* would continue serving the members of the Fellowship as it had before the Council.)

The Council placed the credentialing of "worthy ministers" under Howard Goss, a former assistant to Parham, and T. K. Leonard, director of the Gospel School in

Findlay, Ohio. It recommended two schools: one supervised by R. B. Chisolm near Union, Mississippi, and the other headed by Leonard in Findlay, Ohio.

Some of the delegates chose not to affiliate with the Fellowship. But several hundred ministers transferred their credentials to the new organization. For example, much of the loosely-structured white Church of God in Christ was absorbed by the Assemblies of God.

Among the relatively small group of delegates at Hot Springs were some of the most prominent names in the Pentecostal movement, people whose ministries would touch hundreds of thousands of lives: E. N. Bell, F. F. Bosworth, J. R. Flower, Cyrus Fockler, Howard Goss, D. C. O. Opperman, E. N. Richey, to name a few. Five participants would serve the Assemblies of God as chairman (or, to use the later term, general superintendent): Bell, A. P. Collins, J. W. Welch, W. T. Gaston, Ralph M. Riggs.

In this modest setting, a concern for the conservation of a revival combined with a vision for its expansion—ultimately to shape the Assemblies of God.

3

The Doctrinal Consensus

While some Pentecostals hesitated to participate in organizing efforts, increasing numbers responded favorably to the "cooperative fellowship" concept of the Assemblies of God. By the end of 1914, the ministerial list had increased to 531. In the months following the General Council in Hot Springs, district councils began to form. For his scattered readers E. N. Bell used the *Word and Witness* to develop the Biblical principles for religious "order."

Some situations needed order so desperately that even Charles Parham, as opposed to denominationalism as he was, called the leadership "religious anarchists." They tended to respond to any situation they could not control by saying, "God is not having His way in this meeting. I am going home." Bell agreed that such expressions were far too numerous. Even so, people claimed, "The Holy Ghost has carried on this work for seven years and is able to continue it on, and control it in the future." In response, Bell published articles throughout the summer of 1914 that insisted that Bible order called for cooperation, counsel, and fellowship.

In the course of his efforts to describe "Bible order," Bell made an early try at affirming the beliefs of the Assemblies of God. They included the preaching of salvation, Spirit baptism, spiritual gifts, premillennialism, divine healing; the observance of baptism and Communion; and the gathering of believers in local assemblies. "No rolling or nonsense," he further clarified (in response to the frequent description of Pentecostals as "holy rollers").

In a friendly gesture, he invited all workers willing to spread this "full gospel" to attend the Councils and camps promoted by the General Council of the Assemblies of God. "Nothing was ever more manifestly approved of God," he assured his readers, than the first General Council of the Assemblies of God. The fellowship it had chartered was to be "a servant of the saints; a mere channel through which to work for God's glory; advisory in its capacity, and not a set of bosses."

To some, refraining from a statement of faith was vital. This assured their spiritual freedom. In time, however, it became apparent that the lack of such a statement also jeopardized the Movement. Three doctrinal issues soon demonstrated the need for theological guidelines.

The "Finished Work" of Calvary

Even without an official statement of faith, participants in the Hot Springs General Council clearly leaned toward a concept of salvation that made them open to modifying the Wesleyan-Pentecostal interpretation that was predominant in other organized Pentecostal groups. Wesleyan (or holiness) Pentecostals, like members of the various apostolic faith fellowships or the Pentecostal Holiness Church, taught the need of two "works of grace" before one could be baptized in the Spirit.

In holiness Pentecostal ranks, some claimed that in justification only "actual transgression and guilt" were forgiven; "the heart [remained] full of inbred sin" until the believer experienced a "second definite work of grace." Until this second work, so the teaching went, "enough sin remained in the believer to damn him." To other Pentecostals this seemed to belittle Christ's "finished work" at Calvary.

Among those who rejected the holiness position was William Durham, pastor of Chicago's North Avenue Mission. Born in Kentucky in 1873, Durham had been a Baptist before becoming an independent holiness preacher. He preached and practiced divine healing as well as holy living. When the Pentecostal revival broke out in the Chicago area in 1906, he turned his attention to the Biblical evidence of Spirit baptism. About 50 of his members spoke in tongues at another Chicago mission; they urged their pastor to seek a Pentecostal baptism.

Durham doubted neither their sincerity nor their experience, but he strongly opposed the teaching that tongues were the "uniform initial evidence." Only after lengthy Bible study and careful observation did he acknowledge the validity of the Pentecostal claim. By then he had also admitted, "All the experiences I had ever seen, my own included, were far below the standard God had lifted up in the Acts."

Up to this time he had upheld the teaching that the baptism in the Holy Spirit could be claimed by faith: No evidence was necessary. Now he was deeply challenged. "I could not kneel at the altar, and claim the Holy Ghost and go away," he wrote. "This was a real experience. I must wait until He came." To do so, Durham left for Los Angeles. There he "tarried" for several weeks and then received his Spirit baptism.

After his return to Chicago, Durham's North Avenue Mission became a vibrant Pentecostal center. There E. N. Bell, then a Baptist pastor in Fort Worth, received his Spirit baptism, as did many other seekers. Services, which participants described as marked "by the very presence of God," crowded the facilities. Noise occasionally brought the police. In time, the meetings were noted for the singing of the "heavenly chorus": Those who had been baptized in the Holy Spirit sang in melodic tongues that "echoed and re-echoed across the hall" for an hour or more. Before long, the mission was also a center of controversy, for Durham by 1910 began publicly both to affirm "the finished work of Calvary" and to attack those Pentecostals who taught the "second blessing."

Although many regarded the holiness interpretation of sanctification as a chief Pentecostal truth, Durham said it greatly misrepresented the experience of regeneration. In his point of view the heart was changed at *conversion*: "We are new creatures in Christ through regeneration."

Stated more fully, Durham's message said that "the living faith that justifies a man brings him into Christ, the Sanctifier, in Whom he is complete, not with regard to sanctification only, but [with regard to] everything else that pertains to salvation." The reborn were "saved from sin, death and hell," were "real children of God, possessed of eternal life." They did not need a second work of grace; they needed only "to abide in Christ, receive and walk in the Spirit, hold fast the faith, grow in grace and in the knowledge of God and of Christ." Holiness of heart and life were essential, but such holiness came through "growth in grace" rather than by an instantaneous experience.

Durham was not the only Pentecostal leader who came to these conclusions. A. S. Copley heartily agreed in the pages of the paper he edited, *The Pentecost*. Those who had come into the Pentecostal movement from non-Wesleyan backgrounds were inclined to question the necessity of the "second blessing" and were among the first advocates of the "finished work." Also supporting it were some of the mavericks the movement attracted, people who, like Frank Bartleman, tended to associate with whatever mission seemed to them to have the most recent "revelations."

Because Durham was stubborn and aggressive in his position, much of the storm from the rejection of holiness teaching raged around him. The matter became divisive among those who only 4 years earlier had insisted on their commitment to unity, not only among themselves but also with the Church universal.

Florence Crawford, apostolic faith preacher in Portland, Oregon, labeled the "one work" teaching "a devilish theory from the pit of hell." And even today her followers claim that "this departure from the Word concerning the doctrine of sanctification . . . opened the door for every form of false doctrine." According to them, this has resulted in "one crooked doctrine after another . . . until today the entire movement is honeycombed with conflicting beliefs."

Apostolic faith pioneer Charles Parham accused Durham of preaching "a devil-sent delusion" and of "counting the blood of the covenant an unholy thing." Charging that Durham had "committed the sin unto death," he prayed: "If this man's doctrine is true, let my life go out to prove it; but if our teaching on a definite grace of sanctification is true, let his life pay the forfeit."

For his part, Durham welcomed controversy and opposition as an indication that the Holy Spirit was at work. His language was forceful and uncompromising. The "obvious blessing of God" on his ministry, he claimed, attested the truth of his position. During the heated exchanges, he moved his family to Los Angeles, where he pastored a church of some 600 members. As he put it, he "spoke the plain truth" and "took the consequences." His untimely death on July 7, 1912, however, seemed to vindicate the opposition: Parham noted "how signally" God had answered his prayer.

By 1912, however, "finished work" Pentecostalism already had a strong following. Those who accepted the message gathered in hundreds of unorganized Pentecostal missions across the nation. Some of them associated with the Assemblies of God in 1914. Others formed their own Pentecostal fellowships, such as the Pentecostal Church of God in America. The teaching found almost no acceptance in southern holiness Pentecostal groups or in the early Apostolic Faith centers in Los Angeles, Kansas, and Oregon.

As a result of its policy of cooperative fellowship, the General Council of the Assemblies of God took in some who leaned toward the holiness position. Officially, the Fellowship emphasized both the necessity of holiness and the reality of sanctification. "We believe in getting saved from the dominion of sin," Bell wrote in 1914, "if it takes 40 works."

The "New Issue"

The discussion over the "stages" in salvation occurred just before the organizing of the Assemblies of God. During 1913, another issue appeared which by 1915 would endanger the life of the young Fellowship. At a camp meeting in Arroyo Seco, California, some became fascinated with a "revelation" that exalted the name of Jesus. Before long they would introduce a theology drawn from it. Proponents of a "new issue," they became known as Oneness, or "Jesus only," Pentecostals. As the sanctification controversy had divided American Pentecostalism, so the new issue challenged the Assemblies of God.

To understand this readiness to accept doctrinal "revelations," it is necessary to keep in mind two facts. First,

44

there was a lack of centralized organization in the Pentecostal movement. In some places this situation resulted in the virtual absence of discipline or a standard of authority.

Second, new insights, or revelations, were widely looked upon as indicating spiritual vitality. As apostolic faith preacher Howard Goss said: "A preacher who did not dig up some new slant on a Scripture, or get some new revelation to his own heart ever so often; a preacher who did not propagate it, defend it, and if necessary, be prepared to lay down his life for it, was considered slow, stupid, unspiritual."

Advocates of the new issue unabashedly admitted: "You'll never get this by studying it out like some other doctrine. This comes by revelation!"

A minor influence in entertaining, if not accepting, the new issue may have been the general tendency in the evangelical community to sentimentalize Jesus. Popular gospel songs and preaching failed to include a careful explanation of the Trinity. In the Pentecostal movement, the new awareness of Christ that accompanied the focus on the Holy Spirit made some people overly responsive to so-called revelations about Christ.

At the Arroyo Seco camp meeting, a small group of participants had objected to the selection of the well-established evangelist Maria Woodworth-Etter as main speaker. They desired to see a "forward move" of God rather than to hear Woodworth-Etter's "predictable" message.

As predictable as her message may have been, it likely made an unconscious contribution to the feeling that people needed to be awakened to the power of Jesus' name. The miracles that thrilled her audiences came in response to her prayers "in the name of Jesus."

In any case, two events brought on the crisis. One

John Scheppe claimed a revelation of the power in the name of Jesus. As a result, people studied the Bible on the subject of "the name." They focused on verses like "Do all in the name of the Lord Jesus" and "Whatsoever ye shall ask in my name, that will I do."

Amid this concentration on THE NAME (which, later, often appeared in print in all capital letters), the apostolic baptismal formula in Acts got special notice. In a baptismal service, R. E. McAlister, a Canadian Pentecostal, claimed publicly that the apostles had never used the terms "Father, Son and Holy Ghost" at baptisms but had rather baptized "in the name of Jesus Christ." This view stimulated further discussion of the name.

Apparently everyone at the camp did not share the excitement over these insights. The main speaker, Maria Woodworth-Etter, and several other participants did not mention these events in their accounts of the services.

After the camp meeting, groups of believers along the west coast accepted rebaptism in Jesus' name. Rebaptism was not uncommon among the early Pentecostals; when they discerned some new truth and committed themselves to it, they were rebaptized. (A. J. Tomlinson, leader of the Church of God, for example, was baptized at least three times.) Rebaptism was viewed as leading to greater blessing. Those who had been baptized by sprinkling or pouring often chose to be immersed; those who had been immersed by someone who had not received the baptism in the Holy Spirit occasionally sought rebaptism by one who had received the Spirit.

Gradually, however, a few people began to consider what an emphasis on Jesus' name implied. They examined the healings, miracles, and exorcisms recorded in the New Testament as well as the baptismal formula in Acts 2:38. On the basis of that passage, they concluded that water baptism in the name of Jesus was not optional—it was necessary if one was to be saved. If apostolic Christianity was to be fully restored, the sequence presented there must be followed in the 20th century: water baptism in Jesus' name for the remission of sins, followed by Spirit baptism with the sign of tongues. So water baptism became a basic part of being born again rather than merely an outward sign of an inward work.

Frank Ewart, an Australian who had migrated to Canada and then come to the west coast, began to preach "Jesus only" sermons in which he tried to prove that the Christ of the New Testament was Jehovah of the Old. The terms "Father, Son and Holy Ghost" were titles for *one* Person, Ewart insisted, Jesus. In this way the baptismal formula of Matthew 28—"baptizing them in the *name* of the Father, the Son and the Holy Ghost"—was reconciled with the new teaching. "What is the name?" Ewart would ask. "There is only one person in the Godhead—Jesus Christ," he would answer.

In April 1914 Ewart was pastor of Durham's mission in Los Angeles and one of the most prominent Pentecostals on the west coast. The Wesleyan Pentecostals, however, found him an easy target for criticism. Pointing to his Oneness views, they said such heresy was an outcome of his acceptance of the equally heretical "finished work" teaching. One's lack of a definite "second work," one's denial of crisis sanctification, the argument ran, meant that sin remained in the soul; spiritual confusion and delusion logically followed.

Nonholiness Pentecostals, on the other hand, responded more positively. Not wanting to risk "missing out" on "God's best" for them, some accepted rebaptism in Jesus' name without accepting a denial of the Trinity. Others identified more fully with the evolving "Jesus only" doctrine, trying to spread it throughout the movement.

47

However, when Ewart won over some of the most prominent Pentecostal leaders around the country, earnest orthodox believers concluded that they, too, should accept rebaptism. The confusion that followed immediately affected the Assemblies of God. The optimism and excitement generated at Hot Springs were replaced in 1915 with uncertainty and concern. Rumors of who had—and had not—endorsed the "new issue" abounded, and letters requested E. N. Bell to provide some guidelines in the *Word and Witness*.

Bell and J. R. Flower responded with articles defending Trinitarian views and supporting baptism "in the name of the Father, the Son and the Holy Ghost." Then in July 1915, Bell surprised everyone by accepting rebaptism in Jesus' name at a camp meeting in Tennessee. Within a short time, many Assemblies of God pastors and leaders had followed suit.

When the Third General Council convened in St. Louis, neither the chairman nor the assistant chairman attended the first meeting. It was left to the general secretary, J. R. Flower, to open the session. After 3 days of prayer and testimony, the Council began the difficult task of discussing the "new issue."

Representatives of both sides spoke at length. In the end, the Resolutions Committee proposed accepting both baptismal formulas, but it also formulated a resolution about the distinction of Persons within the Trinity. No decisive action was taken, although the adoption of the Trinitarian resolution encouraged the orthodox faction.

Nevertheless, it became apparent in the next months that further action was needed. Oneness advocates became more aggressive, threatening judgment and ruin for those who resisted their teaching. Their persistent emphasis on revelation over Scripture also troubled many. Their insistence on teaching their controversial doctrine violated the General Council's consensus that new teachings should first be approved by "the brethren." "The Pentecostal movement is now facing a crisis," warned J. R. Flower, "probably the greatest crisis which has ever been and which will ever be in its lifetime."

The newly elected chairman, J. W. Welch, responded by announcing the Fourth General Council for October 1916. Meeting again in St. Louis, the Council would address the need for a Statement of Fundamental Truths that would define for its constituency the accepted doctrines of the Assemblies of God.

The move ran contrary to the intentions of those who had convened in Hot Springs just 30 months earlier; it is a measure of the desperation they felt over the Oneness controversy. Most concluded that such a statement was essential.

When the Council convened, Welch appointed a committee to prepare the statement. One of its members was E. N. Bell, having admitted his error of accepting rebaptism and returned to the Fellowship. Bell had never really endorsed the unorthodox inclinations of Oneness. Rather, he had sincerely hoped to experience more of God by accepting baptism according to the apostolic formula.

D. W. Kerr of Cleveland, Ohio, was responsible for much of the language of the Statement of Fundamental Truths that was presented to the Council. Like Chairman Welch, Kerr was a former member of the Christian and Missionary Alliance. He led the committee in drawing up a detailed section on the Godhead that explicitly excluded the Oneness position. During the sessions, Oneness followers had challenged the right of the Council to formulate a creed. When that failed, they voted against the document, but were unable to block its passage. At the end of the Council, they left in defeat to create their own Oneness Pentecostal fellowships.

Their assertion was essentially a revival of an ancient heresy. Originally it had held that there were no permanent distinctions in the Godhead. One Noetus of Smyrna had claimed, in about A.D. 200, that "Christ was the Father Himself, and that the Father Himself was born, suffered and died." Concerned that their polytheistic culture might see three gods in their beliefs, Monarchians, as they came to be known, introduced a variety of nonorthodox concepts into the Early Church. Their teachings had helped provoke the formulation of the doctrine of the Trinity.

The Statement of Fundamental Truths so effectively expressed the doctrinal consensus of the Assemblies of God that it has remained largely unchanged. During this Oneness crisis, the Assemblies of God was particularly enriched by the contributions of former Christian and Missionary Alliance men, some of whom now replaced Oneness people in positions of leadership. The Statement of Fundamental Truths was largely a statement of conservative evangelical theology and in many ways resembled Alliance thinking. Although it was written to meet a specific need, it became a major step in stabilizing the Assemblies of God.

Those ministers who could not accept the Statement of Fundamental Truths were no longer carried on the rolls of the Fellowship. The ministerial list lost 156 names, reaching a low of 429. But in the Pentecostal movement at large the decisive stand of the General Council of the Assemblies of God in this crisis won the denomination new supporters. Only 2 years later, the number of ministers and missionaries stood at 819.

After this difficult beginning, the Assemblies of God experienced several decades of impressive growth. The adoption of a doctrinal statement made the recurrence of a similar threat unlikely. In the turmoil, the firm and consistent leadership of J. R. Flower and others had given the Movement stability and direction. When a new challenge arose within its ranks in 1917 and 1918, the way it would be addressed had been set in place.

The "Pentecostal Distinctive"

The new problem centered around Fred Francis Bosworth, a popular young evangelist and pastor. Bosworth, a talented musician, had joined the Pentecostal movement in Zion, Illinois, in 1906. He had itinerated widely and had achieved a reputation for success in ministering divine healing. A participant in the Hot Springs convention, Bosworth had many friends at all levels in the Assemblies of God.

During the months following the Oneness crisis, Bosworth began to express frustration over the central Pentecostal position that tongues were the uniform initial evidence of Spirit baptism. This view had helped to define Pentecostalism. Other groups shared other important doctrines of the Pentecostal movement, but the position of evidential tongues was uniquely Pentecostal.

Bosworth also objected to the Pentecostal distinction between tongues as "uniform initial evidence" and tongues as a spiritual gift. He believed that tongues were a gift and functioned as a gift—nothing more.

As a pastor and evangelist, Bosworth was troubled by the way people sought to speak in tongues rather than to be Spirit-filled. "After eleven years in the work on Pentecostal lines," he said, "I am absolutely certain that many who receive the most powerful baptism for service do not receive the manifestation of speaking in tongues."

On the other hand, he believed that many who spoke

in tongues "are not, nor ever have been baptized in the Spirit." "Error in teaching," he concluded, "is mainly responsible for so much of the superficial work and consequent irregularities which Satan has used to turn aside thousands of hungry souls."

Bosworth did not reject speaking in tongues. He concluded rather that any spiritual gift could mean Spirit baptism. This view was shared by members of the Christian and Missionary Alliance, the group with which Bosworth later affiliated.

When Bosworth began to spell out his views and to convince other ministers, letters questioning his teaching poured into the editorial offices of the Assemblies of God paper the *Christian Evangel*. In 1917, the Fifth General Council made it necessary for credentialed ministers to accept the Statement of Fundamental Truths.

In July 1918, Bosworth returned his credentials. Later that year the General Council, meeting for the first time in the new headquarters city of Springfield, Missouri, provided a forum for an open discussion of doctrine. Bosworth attended and was granted permission to address the Council. D. W. Kerr summarized the traditional Pentecostal position, eloquently expressing the scriptural basis for the Movement's distinctive.

In the end, the Council adopted a decisive resolution. "This Council," it read, "considers it a serious disagreement with the Fundamentals for any minister among us to teach contrary to our distinctive testimony that the baptism of the Holy Spirit is regularly accompanied by the initial physical sign of speaking in other tongues as the Spirit of God gives the utterance." Ministers who "attacked as error" this "distinctive testimony" were to be excluded.

The leaders who had fallen under Bosworth's influence were convinced of their mistake. Bosworth himself encouraged them to remain in the Assemblies of God. F. F. Bosworth was a humble, godly man, who maintained good relationships with Pentecostals throughout his long ministry. In 1918, divisive controversy was warded off. Both Bosworth and the General Council of the Assemblies of God remained convinced that Scripture validated their opposing viewpoints: Neither considered compromising what each accepted as New Testament teaching.

By 1918, the infant Fellowship that had emerged in 1914 to promote cooperation and communication had begun its long maturing process. It had withstood serious challenges, spelled out its faith, and set patterns of growth that would continue through the 1920s.

Events had forced a degree of institutionalization that had been unanticipated 4 years before; yet, the conviction that Pentecostalism was a revival movement—a force rather than a family of denominations—held strong. Some deplored the degree of organization. The requirement that ministers accept particular interpretations of Scripture rather than the general authority of Scripture evoked criticism. Independent Pentecostal periodicals reprinted articles by early Pentecostal leaders who had opposed organization; it would "kill the work" as it had, according to William Durham, every other revival in church history.

Those who had outlined the goals of the Assemblies of God and who had, under God, guided the Fellowship through its first difficult years saw the matter differently. They organized prayerfully and decisively, not merely to preserve the revival but to purify and expand it. As a result, the Assemblies of God gained a stability and credibility that contributed to its growth in the United States and around the world.

4

The Developing Outreaches

During its first decade, the Assemblies of God grew significantly and became, in the words of J. R. Flower, a "well-ordered" movement. Hard-won stability attracted members and offered the conditions in which the hopes of the Fellowship's founders began to take shape.

From 1918, the growing ministries of the Assemblies of God were coordinated from a headquarters complex in Springfield, Missouri. Today a headquarters staff of over 900 serves under seven divisions: Christian Education, Church Ministries, Communications, Foreign Missions, Home Missions, Publications, and Treasury. Departments under these divisions coordinate the services the national headquarters offers.

Originally, however, headquarters *was* Gospel Publishing House, and the editorial staff provided the few services available to the Fellowship. The main task was getting out the Pentecostal testimony through the printed page and through the support of missionaries.

Communicating the Good News

Periodicals played a vital role in the early Pentecostal movement. For more than a decade, they held the broader Movement together by keeping worshipers in widely scattered Pentecostal missions aware of their participation in a larger movement. In places having no Pentecostal assemblies, the papers nourished Pentecostal believers.

"Nothing helps our faith like seeing God at work today," noted E. N. Bell. "So let some sober, reliable person in every place where God is working write us the news of the kingdom. Be brief. Exalt Jesus only, and don't exaggerate."

Some of the papers were published occasionally ("as the Lord provides") and sent free upon request. One of the first Pentecostal papers, for example, offered free copies: "If you know of any hungry souls to whom you wish the paper sent," its editor wrote, "send in their addresses and as the Lord permits we will send the paper. We are having 5,000 of this issue printed. The money came in answer to prayer. The next issue will come out as He permits."

Other papers were available regularly and for some there was a small charge. Generally, the papers carried news of the work of God in specific locations, both in the United States and abroad. Through these publications, Pentecostals kept in touch with one another, shared fellowship and insights, asked for prayer, and achieved a sense of family.

Almost every significant leader was associated with a paper. William Piper published the *Latter Rain Evangel*, the Duncan sisters edited *Trust*, Carrie Judd Montgomery published *Triumphs of Faith*, William Durham circulated his "finished work" teaching through the *Pentecostal Testimony*, and several ministries issued separate papers called *Apostolic Faith*.

"The simple tie of fellowship uniting these periodicals," wrote J. R. Flower, "was the common good news that God is now visiting the earth with the outpouring of the Holy Spirit, evidenced by signs and wonders, in preparation for the return of the Lord Jesus Christ."

The Assemblies of God had as its first full-time executives two capable Pentecostal editors, E. N. Bell and J. R. Flower. After receiving the baptism in the Holy Spirit in Chicago, Bell had ministered in Texas and Arkansas. He was a recognized leader in a loose fellowship known as the Church of God in Christ and edited one of the several Pentecostal publications known as the *Apostolic Faith*. When that paper was combined with another called *Word and Witness*, Bell remained editor, keeping for his paper the title *Word and Witness*. His editing, pastoring, and evangelizing prepared him for leadership in the Assemblies of God.

His colleague J. R. Flower had first come across Pentecostalism in an Indianapolis mission when he had stood at the back in amazement as he heard the "heavenly choir." His future wife, Alice Reynolds, recalled an outstanding event of the service: "There was a low murmur of sound from several directions over the congregation. This grew in volume until six persons were on their feet singing in rich harmony a song in the Spirit. Their eyes were closed, but without any confusion these persons moved from their various locations to the front of the hall, where they stood together singing in tongues in beautiful unison, then in harmonizing parts."

Flower, a former cornet player in Zion City's award-winning band, was convinced that this heavenly choir was "of God." He began to seek the Pentecostal experience. He also gave up his study of law and found various ways to work in Christian service. Among these was printing.

Joseph James Roswell Flower got his first two names from his grandfather on his mother's side. Joseph James Rice had been a printer; he had later become a Methodist preacher. His grandson shared his interest in printing and "the urge" came upon him "to publish the good news" of the Pentecostal revival. "It was a venture of faith," he would say, "but the step was taken with the publication of an eight-page monthly entitled simply *The Pentecost* in the fall of 1908." Flower later turned this paper over to a Kansas City minister, A. S. Copley.

In June 1913, Flower and his wife began publishing *The Christian Evangel*. Every week, they produced and mailed it from their home in Plainfield, Indiana, to approximately 1,000 readers.

Those who met at the first General Council in 1914 adopted Bell's *Word and Witness* (then published from his home in Malvern, Arkansas) as the official organ of the Fellowship. But they also gladly accepted Flower's offer of *The Christian Evangel*.

Also at the Hot Springs Council, Evangelist T. K. Leonard volunteered the use of his school facilities in Findlay, Ohio; in June 1914, Bell and Flower moved to Findlay. There they edited and published the *Word and Witness* as a monthly paper and *The Christian Evangel* as a weekly.

The two papers had different formats. The *Word and Witness* contained sermons, testimonies, and reports of camps and revivals. Its chief purpose was the spreading of the Pentecostal message. *The Christian Evangel*, on the other hand, was designed for the needs of a Pentecostal following. A children's page and a Sunday school section supplemented doctrinal and inspirational articles.

Editors Bell and Flower not only edited copy, they wrote and printed it as well. Because of a limited budget, they also serviced their own equipment (such as it was).

Besides urging their readers to support missions, Bell

and Flower served as missions secretaries, forwarding readers' donations to the missionaries they designated.

Both men also taught at Leonard's Gospel School (which the Hot Springs Council had recommended as a training center). The Gospel School was a faith institution. "The students must trust God for their own needs," the announcement read. It was further described as a place where "divinely called men and women can study to show themselves approved unto God." Qualifications for admission included "earnestly waiting upon God for the baptism of the Holy Ghost, the gifts of the Spirit, or a proper place in the body of Christ; and those seeking the knowledge of the Word."

But the growth of their publishing efforts and related responsibilities soon called for larger facilities.

Toward the end of 1914, Bell and Flower asked for a second General Council, "to lay a firm foundation upon which to build the fellowship of the Assemblies of God."

This Council met at the Stone Church in Chicago in November. The Stone Church was a well-known assembly in the early Pentecostal movement. Its regular conventions and monthly paper, *The Latter Rain Evangel*, made it a center of activity. Located in Chicago where all missionaries and evangelists going east or west had to change trains because there was no cross-country service, the church attracted the ministry of the best-known Pentecostal leaders.

The Stone Church, like most other Pentecostal assemblies, proclaimed healing. Publicity about healings became a factor in the church's rapid growth. The congregation also maintained a typical early Pentecostal faith home. Opened "for all who wish to seek some definite blessing from Him," it was advertised as a home "for both well and sick; for those who are seeking sanctification, the baptism in the Holy Spirit, healing or any other of our Father's gracious blessings."

In this strong and popular Pentecostal center, the second General Council addressed its growth needs. Its ministerial list now included 522 ministers, evangelists, and missionaries.

Archibald P. Collins, a Pentecostal leader from northern Texas, replaced Bell as chairman, but Bell remained editor of publications. J. R. Flower was named office editor. Among the many decisions the Council made, none had more long-term effects than the authorization to raise at least $5,000 to purchase publishing equipment.

After the Council, Gospel Publishing House moved from Findlay to St. Louis, where a donated press and some secondhand equipment were installed in the building housing the headquarters offices. Those who served in the publishing house and the headquarters shared a large home leased from the Salvation Army. It had two-room apartments for married couples and rooms for single workers. It also served a steady stream of guests (even though it was in an undesirable part of the city).

During the Oneness crisis that disturbed the Fellowship in the next 2 years, Bell gave up his editing responsibilities. For several months, Office Editor J. R. Flower performed all the editorial duties. Then John William Welch was elected chairman and assumed the accompanying editorial responsibilities. At about this time, *Word and Witness* ceased publication, and *The Christian Evangel* became the sole paper of the Fellowship. For a time, it was known as the *Weekly Evangel*. Then to bear witness to its Pentecostal position, the October 18, 1919, issue was introduced as the *Pentecostal Evangel* (which it has remained).

The years in St. Louis were marked by thrift. "If those

early workers had not sacrificed," said one, "the Gospel Publishing House would have gone on the rocks." Another of them recalled one of the crises: "We owed $1,800 and Brother Flower said we simply must have a new folding machine that would cost $400. So we knelt together and prayed for $2,000. . . . But the Lord . . . knew we would need more than that . . . so He put it on the heart of a lady in San Diego to send $3,000." The faith and vision of the early staff carried the work forward.

By 1917, more room was again needed. The next year, Gospel Publishing House and the headquarters offices moved to Springfield, Missouri.

Meanwhile, Chairman Welch had been struggling with his editing duties. Untrained for such work, he felt inadequate. In 1916, he requested friends to pray for "God's man" for the paper; he also invited Stanley Frodsham to attend that year's Council and accept being considered for a headquarters assignment.

Frodsham, a young Englishman, had participated in the British Pentecostal revival that had centered in Sunderland between 1907 and 1914. A talented preacher and writer, Frodsham was aware of the moving of the Holy Spirit throughout the world. He also had editing experience, having published in England a Pentecostal paper known as *Victory*. He accepted Welch's invitation to the 1916 General Council. But most of those present knew him only by his articles in Pentecostal papers.

At the General Council, Chairman Welch met Mary Arthur, through whose healing the Pentecostal movement had been established in southern Kansas in 1903. An ordained minister, she was highly respected, and Welch asked her, "Have you been praying for God's man to be the editor of the *Evangel?*"

"Yes," she responded, "and every time I pray, the Lord shows me that the man who wrote this article is the one He has chosen." She pointed to an article that had appeared the previous week in the *Evangel*. It was by Frodsham. Welch appreciated the confirmation of his own impression.

To Frodsham's surprise, the Council chose him to serve as general secretary. He also participated on the committee that drafted the Statement of Fundamental Truths. For several years he served as general secretary and as missionary treasurer while assisting Welch in his editing duties.

In 1919 the General Council named J. T. Boddy editor. He was a respected older pastor who had come into the Assemblies of God from the Christian and Missionary Alliance. But his poor health forced Frodsham to assume much of the work. When Frodsham finally became editor in his own right in 1921, he had been well prepared. Except for a brief interval (1928-1929), he served for nearly 30 years as editor of the *Pentecostal Evangel*. (For most of those years, he was also general editor for all Gospel Publishing House materials.)

Frodsham was widely read and intellectually alert. He was ably assisted after 1925 by several associate editors: chief among them was Charles Elmo Robinson. Robinson (a former lawyer and pastor) and his wife, Daisy, began their long association with the *Evangel* staff in the following way:

In 1925, Daisy Robinson's health called for a change in their circumstances. They prayed, Charles Robinson recalled, that "God would send me to the Gospel Publishing House . . . where I could draw a salary and so make the living, and she be free from responsibility. . . . We agreed that we would not make any sort of an application for a position in Springfield. We wanted our going there . . . to be surely in the will of God."

A few weeks later, the General Council met in nearby

Eureka Springs. Robinson, 58 years old, had never met any Assemblies of God officials. He attended the Council,. which adopted a resolution to employ an associate editor. "As soon as the resolution was passed," Robinson recalled, "Brother Frodsham hurriedly left the platform and came directly to me. He placed his hand on my shoulder and said, without a word of introduction or preface, 'You are the man I want for associate editor.' "

The Robinsons made a rich contribution to the Assemblies of God in both preaching and writing, and Mr. Robinson served the organization as legal consultant as well.

When Frodsham resigned as editor in 1949, Robert Cunningham, who had assisted Frodsham since 1937, assumed the responsibilities of editor. He and Robinson worked together until Robinson's death in 1954. On Cunningham's retirement in 1984, Richard G. Champion, longtime associate editor, became *Evangel* editor.

The overlapping service of these men, plus their spiritual vitality and long tenure, has provided continuity that has benefited the *Pentecostal Evangel* and, through it, the entire Fellowship.

As the Fellowship grew, gifted men and women within it began to write doctrinal and devotional literature as well as Sunday school material from a specifically Pentecostal point of view. Gospel Publishing House became the major Pentecostal publisher.

Radio

At the end of World War II, the national offices of the Assemblies of God began serious efforts to use radio to carry the gospel. The 1945 General Council set up a Radio Department and accepted from California Pastor Leland Keys an offer of the radio ministry he had launched in the west. The first broadcast of the pilot program, *Sermons in Song*, in January 1946 featured General Superintendent Ernest Williams as speaker and Thomas F. Zimmerman as narrator.

In April 1950, the Radio Department introduced a new half-hour format for the broadcast and changed its name to *Revivaltime*. General Superintendent Wesley Steelberg was the speaker until his death in 1952. Several others assisted in the ministry. Then the 1953 General Council voted to select a full-time speaker, to produce the broadcast live, and to release it through a major network.

Charles Morse Ward, son of Canadian Pentecostal pioneer A. G. Ward, was the unanimous choice of the Executive Presbytery for radio speaker. He began his 25-year association with *Revivaltime* in December 1953 on the ABC network. Having an evangelistic rather than denominational emphasis, *Revivaltime* has nevertheless helped acquaint people with the Assemblies of God.

When Ward retired in 1978, Evangelist Dan Betzer followed him. *Revivaltime* is now carried on 565 stations and is aired in over 100 countries. The promotion of prayer through a 24-hour prayerline, the Radio Prayer Partner Fellowship, and World Prayer Meetings has been vital to its growth.

Communicating the Pentecostal message is paramount to the Assemblies of God, just as it was in 1914. And just as *Word and Witness* kept the Fellowship in touch with itself, so radio has joined print ministry in this vital role—which today offers the added awareness of the world at large.

Providing Pentecostal Education

Pentecostalism arose in a religious culture that stressed

knowing Scripture, and it was rooted in the Biblical literalism of one segment of late 19th-century evangelicalism.

Some early Pentecostal leaders had had formal ministerial training in well-established, accredited programs. Many more had attended one of the Bible institutes (like Simpson's or Moody's) where they were prepared for practical ministries.

The programs in these schools emphasized mastery of the English Bible and the use of gospel songs in evangelism. These schools sent their students out daily to do evangelistic work.

The unique Pentecostal teaching on speaking in tongues as evidence of the baptism in the Holy Spirit had been prepared at another kind of Bible school. It was less formal, with few instructors or texts. Such schools sometimes had only one teacher and used only the Bible. These schools stressed prayer and religious experience. Teachers and students tried to pray into their lives the truths they discussed.

Such Bible schools were often short-term, although some became well established. As the Pentecostal movement grew, Charles Parham helped spread it to new locations by conducting short-term apostolic faith Bible schools in several places in the south central states.

In places where many Christians were unfamiliar with Pentecostalism, such schools served the Movement well. Bible schools, lasting from several weeks to several months, and moving from one location to another, furnished teaching and inspiration.

Often schools were founded where a Pentecostal revival was occurring. Instruction was tempered with openness to the Spirit of God. The schools were centers of charismatic Christianity in action.

For the Assemblies of God, one of the most important

pioneer educators in the early Pentecostal movement was D. C. O. Opperman, a former schoolteacher and administrator. In 1905, he left his formal school duties in Dowie's Zion City for full-time ministry.

To better equip himself for Pentecostal evangelism, he attended a short-term Bible institute in Waco, Texas, and eventually became Texas state director of the Apostolic Faith Movement. At the beginning of 1909, he included educational opportunities in his evangelistic ministry.

Opperman's first short-term school in Texas was described as a faith school: "no charges for board, room, or tuition." Students were expected to contribute to a common fund from which "we shall trust God to supply all needs."

Its practical emphasis was also made clear: "In connection with the Bible school," the announcement read, "an evangelistic meeting will be conducted every night. There will also be street, shop, and prison meetings in connection with the school." During the first years of the Pentecostal revival, hundreds of Pentecostals went from such schools "into the Pentecostal harvest field."

More and more, however, the training at short-term schools seemed inadequate. Some people saw a need for standardizing these schools and expanding their influence. This could be done, so the thinking went, by making them permanent institutions where young people could get systematic training for ministry in an atmosphere prepared by the Holy Spirit.

Advocates of systematized education, however, had to approach the subject carefully. The widespread conviction of Christ's soon return made education seem a waste of time to some people. Others feared a tendency to stress academic training more than spiritual sensitivity. Recalling their experiences in the "dead" denominational churches around them, some Pentecostals thought of education as irrelevant to the practical and overwhelming task of evangelism. Since the things of the Spirit were "revealed by the Spirit" and could not be comprehended by "the natural man," these people reasoned, formal training for ministry was unnecessary.

In a few locations, small permanent Bible institutes were set up to complement the ministries of local assemblies. For example, Bethel Pentecostal Tabernacle, under its pastor, Allan Swift, opened Bethel Bible Institute in Newark, New Jersey, in 1916. Glad Tidings Bible Institute grew out of the new converts class of a San Francisco mission. Opened in 1919, it was approved by the General Council in the same year.

At the same time, leaders considered sponsoring a Fellowship school and proposed locating it in the Midwest. In 1920, the General Council of the Assemblies of God joined several of its districts in sponsoring the Mid-West Bible School at Auburn, Nebraska, and urged all Assemblies of God churches to support it. But difficulties beset the small school from its beginning. It seemed impossible to find adequate, qualified faculty. Opening day had to be delayed twice: once because of a coal strike and then because of an epidemic—during which the mayor quarantined the city. Critical financial needs could not be met. Although the Fellowship promoted the Nebraska school, it had only 2 of the 11 votes on the school's board of directors. The Fellowship's leaders decided that the venture lacked "the providential confirmation that attends the true leading of the Lord."

The next year, leaders decided to open a school for which they had full responsibility. They agreed to locate it in Springfield. They accepted as "confirmation" the donating of 15 acres of land in north Springfield to the Fellowship for a Bible school.

Daniel Warren Kerr, by this time affectionately known as "Daddy Kerr" within the Movement, had long dreamed of a Bible school administered by the General Council of the Assemblies of God. His daughter recalled his saying: "I feel like Simeon of old. If I could just see a Bible school in Springfield, I could say, Now lettest Thou Thy servant depart in peace."

Kerr had been a pioneer of the Pentecostal movement. In 1907, while pastoring the Christian and Missionary Alliance Tabernacle in Dayton, Ohio, he heard of the Azusa Street revival and began "to dig into the Word of God to find out 'whether these things be so.' " At that summer's camp meeting on the Christian and Missionary Alliance conference grounds, a Pentecostal revival broke out and Kerr and his wife "came through to a beautiful baptism of the Holy Spirit."

Four years later, Kerr accepted a Christian and Missionary Alliance pastorate in Cleveland, Ohio.

Since most of the congregation had received Spirit baptism, they voted to become Pentecostal. Kerr brought with him into Pentecostal ministry a vision for evangelism and education nourished by years of work with Alliance founder A. B. Simpson. This included commitment to Bible training.

Kerr had helped in the development of other Bible schools sponsored by local Assemblies of God churches. Twice, in critical General Council sessions, he had been a key figure in defining Assemblies of God doctrine: in 1916 during the Oneness crisis and in 1918 during the discussion of the initial evidence of Spirit baptism.

Kerr gladly accepted Chairman E. N. Bell's invitation to supervise the new school, to be known as Central Bible Institute. In the fall of 1922, classes began in the basement of Springfield's Central Assembly of God. There were no dormitories; students roomed with church members.

At the 1923 General Council, the Executive Presbytery was appointed a Bible school commission and made responsible for the supervision of the growing number of Bible schools associated with the various districts of the Assemblies of God. Efforts were made to standardize the programs at the several local schools. And leaders urged the constituency to support the various Bible schools.

There was also an increasing commitment to liberal arts education. The 1929 General Council adopted a report that concluded:

> On account of the worldliness of many of our high schools and colleges and their antagonistic attitude for the most part to the Pentecostal message, there is a growing need of academic schools of our faith in different parts of our country to provide education without contamination of worldly and anti-Christian influences. We believe that our fellowship should look with favor upon the establishment of such schools, and should look forward to the time, if the Lord tarry, when we may have somewhere an institution of college grade, where the most complete and thorough education can be obtained under Pentecostal auspices.

Events related to World War II pressured Assemblies of God schools to broaden and update their curricula, to pursue accreditation, and to grant recognized degrees. The specific requirements for military chaplains, for example, included substantial academic work. After Central Bible Institute made a fourth and fifth year of work available in 1947, the institute was granted accreditation by the Accrediting Association of Bible Colleges. In 1965 it was renamed Central Bible College.

Over the years, several smaller regional schools merged with CBC. It remains the only resident Bible college operated by the General Council of the Assemblies of God.

The 1945 General Council created a Department of Education with three divisions: Church School, Academic, and Bible Institute. The Church School Division was closely related to the Sunday school ministry of Gospel Publishing House. The Academic Division supervised Christian day schools and considered what the founding of a liberal arts college might mean. The Bible Institute Division included supervision of the various institutes as well as a program launched by Frank Boyd in 1947 known as the Berean School.

Boyd (also trained for ministry at the Christian and Missionary Alliance school in Nyack, New York) devised a correspondence program for ministers unable to attend one of the Bible institutes and for lay people. Over the years, it has grown remarkably. In 1984 it offered 52 courses and had an enrollment of 37,049, over half of whom were laypeople.

Early in 1985, the Executive Presbytery authorized the incorporation of the Berean School into a college, Berean College of the Assemblies of God. Designed as a nontraditional college, it will offer three levels of training: college degree courses, courses directed toward preparation for ministerial credentialing, and classes to enrich students who need neither degrees nor credentials.

The intermittent interest in liberal arts education finally came together in the 1950s under the executive leadership of Ralph M. Riggs.

The quest had been long and difficult. The General Presbytery had approved the creation of a liberal arts college in 1944, but the General Council had not followed suit. While committees worked on the project, more requests came from the constituency for such a school.

World War II renewed interest in setting up a liberal arts college. Stories of young people "lost to the fellowship" because they attended secular colleges multiplied. "Our church is crippling itself by losing so many of our good young people . . . in allowing them to be educated in other colleges," reported the planning committee.

Ralph Riggs (then an assistant general superintendent) made a survey of the Bible schools which found that about 35 percent of the students felt no call to ministry. They were clearly not "preparing themselves for their chosen life work in this manner"; some, the report asserted, develop " 'a preacher's complex' from such training and environment and become misfits."

Although the committee offered ways to assure such a college's loyalty to the Movement, the General Council defeated the proposal. The opposition represented various opinions in the constituency. Some feared liberal arts training, citing instances in which church-related liberal arts schools had become spiritually dead. Others agreed with the anti-intellectualism that had strongly appealed to some early Pentecostals. Still others thought the whole matter irrelevant because they expected Christ's immediate return.

Meanwhile, circumstances had become favorable for getting an attractive piece of government land—O'Reilly General Hospital, built for Army use during World War II. Fellowship leaders began the application process. In December 1954, the land—nearly 60 acres, with 70 semipermanent buildings—was given to the organization, a 100-percent discount. In 1953, the General Council had finally authorized a liberal arts school. Evangel College opened in 1955 with 88 students. In 1965, the North Central Accrediting Association granted the school full accreditation.

Evangel College students are trained for a wide variety

of lay and pastoral world outreach ministries. Committed to the preparation of the whole person—spiritually, intellectually, and physically—for practical Christian witness, the college seeks to balance academic excellence with spiritual integrity.

A growing membership's changing needs and society's increasing stress on higher education suggested the usefulness of an Assemblies of God graduate studies program. After it was considered at length, the Assemblies of God Graduate School (renamed Assemblies of God Theological Seminary in 1984) opened in the headquarters complex in the fall of 1973.

Accredited by the North Central Accrediting Association, the seminary grants both master of arts and master of divinity degrees. A growing extension program brings graduate-level training to hundreds who are unable to come to Springfield.

Most of the schools endorsed by the General Council of the Assemblies of God have advanced from Bible institutes to Bible colleges. Many have also added liberal arts training and now offer accredited bachelor's degrees.

Over the years, the number and character of endorsed programs have changed. The current list of endorsed colleges (in addition to the nationally supported schools) includes Bethany Bible College (Santa Cruz, California), North Central Bible College (Minneapolis), Northwest College of the Assemblies of God (Kirkland, Washington), Southeastern College of the Assemblies of God (Lakeland, Florida), Southern California College (Costa Mesa), Southwestern Assemblies of God College (Waxahachie, Texas), Trinity Bible College (Ellendale, North Dakota), Valley Forge Christian College (Phoenixville, Pennsylvania).

Besides the accredited colleges, there are five endorsed Bible institutes, four of which are concerned with ethnic ministries.

Many within the Assemblies of God have come to accept and appreciate the role formal education can have in helping to equip the membership for practical ministry and effective Christian witness.

5

The Evangelism Imperative

From its beginnings, the Assemblies of God has been committed to proclaiming the gospel at home and abroad. Evangelism is part of its reason for being.

At the turn of the century, many American Protestants showed renewed interest in both foreign and home missions. The Student Volunteer Movement enlisted thousands of young people on America's campuses in "the evangelization of the world in this generation." Liberal and conservative Protestants alike sensed a Christian obligation to their own society and other cultures.

Wherever the premillennialist hope—central to early Pentecostalism—was proclaimed, it sparked interest in evangelism. In the late 19th century, those who had become convinced that Christ's return was near had been roused to seek power to win their world to Christ.

The hope of Christ's soon return served the cause of evangelism in at least two ways. It aroused concern for lost souls. It also caused some to believe that missions played a part in bringing about Christ's coming: "This gospel . . . shall be preached in all the world," they read in Matthew 24, ". . . then shall the end come."

Probably no subject came up more often in the early Pentecostal movement than the return of Christ. "Jesus is coming," exhorted a Los Angeles Pentecostal in 1906. "Go forward . . . preach the Gospel of the Kingdom, for the King's business demands haste." Alice Reynolds Flower expressed the feeling of the time in verse:

Have I forgotten that Jesus is coming?
Have I forgotten my part in it all?
Lord, help Thy servant to fail Thee no longer,
Though it is late, I go at Thy call.

This hope, suggesting missions responsibility, lent itself particularly well to the Pentecostal experience of Spirit baptism. The Baptism was "enduement with power for service." It obligated recipients to serve. And it empowered them to proclaim Christ effectively.

For several decades before the Assemblies of God was formed, non-Pentecostals had understood their task largely in "Pentecostal" terms. When the Pentecostal movement appeared, giving unusual force to earlier evangelical ideas, a vibrant missions emphasis followed naturally.

Evangelism Abroad

American Pentecostal foreign missions had two major sources of support. The first was the Pentecostal revival in the homeland. The baptism in the Holy Spirit tended to stimulate interest in missions. Challenged with the needs of a lost and soon-to-be-judged world, Spirit-baptized people sought opportunities for service.

The second source was the Pentecostal revival on the mission fields. In some cases, missionaries read accounts of the meetings at Azusa Street and elsewhere. In others, influential Pentecostals traveled to the mission fields and won over missionaries of all denominations.

Still other events supported the claim that the Pentecostal revival was part of a spontaneous worldwide awakening. "News comes from India that the baptism with the Holy Ghost and gift of tongues is being received there by natives who are simply taught of God," the Azusa Street mission reported. "Communities are being stirred and transformed by the wonderful grace of God. Healing, the gift of tongues, visions, dreams, discernment of spirits, the power to prophesy and to pray the prayer of faith all have a place in the present revival."

Just as itinerant evangelists multiplied in the United States as the revival spread, so the ranks of those who felt a call to the foreign field grew. Many thrilling stories of guidance and provision mark this early chapter in Pentecostal missions.

John Lake, who took the Apostolic Faith Mission to South Africa, for example, had no money as he prepared to leave for South Africa with a group of coworkers. "I needed $2,000," he recalled, "and had not one cent. In answer to prayer—private prayer in my own room—an unknown donor from Monrovia, California, a place I had never visited, sent . . . four five-hundred dollar drafts saying: 'While I was in the bank today, God said to me, "Send Lake $2,000. It is needed for a special purpose."' "

With the money for transportation provided, Lake and his party left for South Africa in May 1908. Before they could leave the ship, however, they needed $125 in cash "to put up with the Immigration Department." "I had not a cent," Lake reported. "As I stood in the line of people who were making payments, awaiting my chance to explain to the immigration officer my dilemma, suddenly a man tapped me on the shoulder, called me out of the line, handed me a traveler's check for $200 and said to me, 'I feel led to give you this to help in your work.' "

On the other hand, major problems similar to those at home did develop on the foreign field.

Missionaries usually went to the mission field in faith, with no boards and often no stable congregations behind them. The urgency of their compassion for souls made the matters of support and training seem unimportant.

Some used the language they thought they had been given at their Spirit baptism to decide what field to go to. In October 1906, for example, the *Apostolic Faith* reported on a young woman's "consecration for Africa": "I am saved, sanctified and baptized with the Holy Ghost and have the Bible evidence. The Lord showed me that the language I spoke was the language of Africa." The paper also reported that a Sister Hutchins had "received the baptism with the Holy Ghost and the gift of the Uganda language." She and her husband set out for Africa with their niece (who, they claimed, had "also been given the African language.") Those sincerely desiring to serve urgently needed stability and direction.

Among the aims of the General Council at Hot Springs in 1914 was the organizing of the Pentecostal missionary efforts. In issuing the call to meet at Hot Springs, Bell had identified these purposes: "a better understanding of the needs of the foreign field and . . . the concentration of means and methods for more efficient missionary work."

The first General Council took seriously its obligation to evangelism. It authorized its Executive Presbytery to serve as a Home and Foreign Missions Presbytery. The presbytery's specific duties included help in forwarding funds; counseling with departing missionaries; the legal holding of property purchased abroad with missionary money (with the added obligation of assuring "that it is not alienated from the Pentecostal cause of God").

Several missionaries attended the Hot Springs Council; others wrote from the field in the following months wanting to affiliate. During 1914, from the Gospel Publishing House, Editors Bell and Flower handled the missionary funds sent by individuls and churches. They forwarded all of the moneys sent in, taking out nothing for expenses. Designated funds were sent to the appropriate missionary whether or not he had joined the Assemblies of God.

Bell and Flower served the missions cause in another important way. Their publications kept the needs of missionaries before the Fellowship and prodded its members to support evangelism with prayer and finances. "If there ever was a time when our people should pray and get hold of God for the dear missionaries in the foreign lands, it is just now," read a typical paragraph. "Try by all means to have funds reach us before the end of the month. Do not neglect or delay to send at any and all times." The magazines also kept the missionaries aware of the Movement's progress at home.

By the second General Council, in November 1914, the editors had forwarded some $10,000 to missionaries.

The 1915 Council passed a resolution about the "testing," sending, supporting, and supervising of missionaries. It set up guidelines for getting qualified personnel and making a missions work effective. After giving evidence of their religious experience, missionary candidates were to be endorsed by their local churches. If they had no local affiliation, thcy needed the recommendation of five executive presbyters "as to Christian standing."

The Oneness controversy disrupted missionary giving, but after 1917, funds began to increase steadily. In 1919 General Secretary J. R. Flower could report that enough income had been received to send out all the qualified, available workers. The Assemblies of God missionary force numbered 195. The entire list of ordained ministers at home and abroad had grown to 831.

Much of the work of the 1919 General Council was devoted to foreign missions. "The 1919 General Council," wrote J. R. Flower, "completed an era of progress which firmly established the Assemblies of God as an aggressive agency for foreign missionary work." The Council separated foreign missions from the office of publications and created a foreign missions department. Flower became the department's first secretary-treasurer. By writing and preaching, he faithfully publicized the needs of missions and planned for its advance.

The Council report noted the continuing importance of the *Evangel* to the missions cause. Readers gave an average of $5 each to missions. Largely through Gospel Publishing House efforts, $96,973.59 had been received and distributed. The Council urged local assemblies to promote subscriptions to the *Evangel* as a way of supporting missions.

During these formative years, Assemblies of God missions policy began to develop. Flower encouraged the idea of the self-supporting church and the training of national workers. Missionaries founded Bible schools wherever possible. Because of this farsightedness, the work of the Assemblies of God would be able to continue during later nationalistic turmoil. National pastors were trained in national schools to lead their own fellowships. The missionary was not irreplaceable.

The number of Bible schools abroad has continued to increase. Today, 250 overseas Bible schools enroll about 22,000 students.

A careful reading of early missions policies reveals some of the problems early administrators faced. To make sure local churches developed programs supporting missions, missionaries were discouraged from making "promiscuous and independent itineraries." It became necessary to formally disapprove of "all floating missionary efforts" and of "all aimless travel from place to place instead of settling down to learn the language and opening up stations and doing permanent missionary work."

Flower also began setting up budgets for all missionaries. He calculated in 1921 that at least $40 a month was needed to support each missionary, children and travel representing additional funds. He estimated that each mission station required between $25 and $30 for monthly maintenance. Projected annual need stood at $233,800.

The problem was complicated by those who marked their offering for a particular missionary, causing an unequal distribution of funds among the missionaries. But the greater problem was simply the lack of money. Flower recalled the difficulty of deciding where to send offerings marked "for the neediest missionary." "This designation," he said, "would apply to two-thirds of the missionaries on our list."

After about 10 years (long after Flower had left office), missionary giving reached a level that allowed the Fellowship to carry out Flower's budget plans. But throughout the 1920s Assemblies of God missionaries often failed to average $40 monthly income. The reports they sent back, however, were filled with stories of God's provision for their needs.

After various administrative changes occurred, Noel Perkin assumed the leadership of Assemblies of God foreign missions in 1927. He guided the department until his retirement in 1959 and was known throughout the Fellowship as Mr. Missions.

A more dedicated leader could not have been found. His service as a missionary and a pastor, his years of bookkeeping experience in banking, his spiritual fervor—all combined for the advancement of missions at home and abroad.

. Born in the northern part of London, England, Perkin was raised in the Wesleyan Methodist Church. He attended a boarding school in Cambridge run by a former Methodist missionary to China.

As a young man, he accepted a job with the Bank of Montreal in Canada. He spent over 7 years in banking. In spite of success, he lacked spiritual fulfillment. "Life," he recalled, "looked so empty."

At length he moved to a boarding house run by a woman who had been a missionary to South America. Under the influence of this family, he reported, "I began reaching out for something to satisfy my spiritual nature. . . . At about this time I was introduced to Pentecostal people who were assembling mostly in small cottage meetings and a rented hall." One of the groups was led by C. H. Schoonmaker (missionary, and father of a family of Assemblies of God missionaries). Like the Schoonmakers, Perkin had thrived on the ministry of A. B. Simpson in the Christian and Missionary Alliance. In various ways, then, he had been exposed to missions and influenced by missionaries throughout his life.

Perkin began to seek the baptism in the Holy Spirit. Soon after he had received the Spirit, he and a friend rented a hall and sponsored evangelistic services. The result was a congregation of about 600 believers who began to reach out in missions. There Perkin "stepped out in faith" and declared his own call to the foreign field. Ordination followed, and he left his employment, launching a faith ministry. "I had no promise of support other than the assurance that my friends . . . would most likely stand back of me as far as they were able," he recalled. He made arrangements to go to South America. Experiences as a pioneer missionary in Argentina added to his preparation for the executive leadership he would later give to missions.

After a time, he returned to the United States to spend some time at the Elim Bible Training School in Rochester, New York, where he "sought God's mind" for his future. There he met and married Ora Blanchard. They accepted a call to a pastorate.

In 1926 he felt that a change in his ministry was approaching. The next mail brought an invitation to assist in the business management of the Gospel Publishing House. "I have a quiet feeling that this offer is of God," he told his wife. A year after his arrival in Springfield, he accepted the office of missions secretary-treasurer. For the next 33 years, "he lived, ate, drank, talked, dreamed and sacrificed for missions."

In the 1920s, programs supporting missions and offering special ministries were organized. The newly formed Women's Missionary Council (now Women's Ministries) had among its purposes the spreading of the gospel and assisting of missions. Programs such as Spanish publications were developed. Today this ministry has expanded to include literature in other languages as well and is known as LIFE International. Speed-the-Light called on youth to raise money for equipment for missionaries. The Boys and Girls Missionary Crusade, introduced in 1949, collected offerings for missions. In 1957 Light-for-the-Lost began to provide evangelism literature. These programs, coordinated under various divisions, give vital support to missionary evangelism and education efforts.

During Noel Perkin's administration, the Assemblies of God missionary force included some outstanding individuals recognized by secular authorities for their humanitarian activities. Among them were two women, Lillian Trasher, who founded an orphanage in Assiout,

Egypt, and Florence Steidel, who developed New Hope Town to minister to Liberian lepers.

Steidel went to Liberia as a missionary nurse in 1935. Deeply moved by the condition of the lepers she met daily, she dreamed of building a home for them. During her second furlough from the field she took a college course in elementary construction. When she returned to Liberia in 1944, she began an outpatient program for lepers.

Her decision to allow one leper to build a bush house at the mission station attracted others. When 68 had built huts, Steidel put her knowledge of construction to use. She began with mud-brick houses, and later added permanent buildings. The settlement was called New Hope Town.

In time, New Hope Town included a clinic, children's homes (for infected children and for children whose parents were receiving treatment), schools, and a farm. She trained nationals to run the clinic, and she helped patients learn trades like carpentry and brickmaking.

Thousands of lepers received help and hope at New Hope Town. More importantly, 90 percent of those treated at her clinic received Christ.

At Liberia's centennial celebration in April 1957, President William Tubman surprised Florence Steidel by announcing: "There is a lady in this audience who is worthy of decoration." Tubman conferred on her the decoration of Knight Official of the Humane Order of African Redemption.

Most of the missionaries, however, won no such acclaim. Nevertheless, they faithfully fulfilled their call; this was demonstrated by the Movement's impressive growth.

Over the years, the expansion of the missions program has called for administrative changes. Field directors, field coordinators, and area representatives have assumed a large share of the responsibility that once rested solely on the missions secretary.

Noel Perkin retired in 1959. His successor, J. Philip Hogan, has expanded earlier programs and developed new strategies to promote missions.

Traditional overseas Bible schools have been supplemented by the International Correspondence Institute, which over the years has enrolled 12 million students in 164 countries. MAPS (Mobilization and Placement Service) coordinates teams of lay people who contribute their services for completion of specific missions-related building projects. Ambassadors-in-Mission sends college-age young people to the mission field as summer interns, and appoints others to special tasks abroad.

Throughout the years, preaching the gospel has remained the priority of Assemblies of God missions. This has not meant ignoring other needs, however. Missionaries continue to compassionately reach out to ease the suffering around them. Mark Buntain's work in Calcutta, for example, includes schools, feeding programs, and a hospital, as well as preaching stations. Directly and through other agencies, Assemblies of God funds have supported relief projects and refugee ministries. Recently, a new outreach, Health Care Ministries, has been organized.

As a fellowship, the Assemblies of God remains committed to the premillennialism that prompted the earliest Pentecostal missionary efforts. It affirms the lost condition of all who are without Christ. In one sense, the missionary outreach, abroad and at home, is a measure of how true the Movement has been to its heritage.

Evangelism at Home

In the early history of the Assemblies of God, overseas

evangelism received more formal attention than home missions. The constituency did not think of their various local evangelistic outreaches in terms of "home missions." Involvement was, in a sense, assumed. Evangelists itinerated, converts pioneered churches, and the Fellowship grew without programs or planned activities.

The Executive Presbytery, as created in 1914, was also the Home and Foreign Missionary Presbytery. But most of its work related to the foreign fields.

In 1919, however, the General Council passed a resolution urging that the district councils "press the work" of "carrying the Pentecostal Message into the neglected districts of the country." "Brethren who felt led" to do so were authorized to evangelize in such areas, and the executives agreed to consult with evangelists about "pushing out into new fields."

In the beginning, much of the actual responsibility for home missions was left to the districts. But interest in a more systematic approach to home missions continued to be expressed at General Councils. The 1921 Council began a fund for home missions. As was the case with foreign missions, appeals through the *Evangel* were important to the raising of home missions support. It soon became evident that the foreign missions outreach depended on strengthening the home base: Home and foreign missions were inseparable.

Not until the 1937 Council did home missions achieve departmental status. In that year it was attached to the Education Department. Fred Vogler became the first executive officer of the Education and Home Missions Department.

Although Vogler's term of office was brief, his record was impressive. He was a true pioneer of Pentecost. Born in Australia in 1888, he had migrated to Zion City with his parents in 1905. When he became involved with the

Pentecostal revival in Zion City, he made a wholehearted commitment to Christ and began to engage in Christian work.

Early in 1908, he began full-time ministry, traveling with others as an evangelist. "We would go to a town not knowing where we would stay or where the meetings would be held," he recalled. "We had no advance manager, no capital. . . . But God gave us the victory."

After years of pioneer ministry, Vogler became Kansas District Superintendent. "The Assemblies of God work in Kansas prospered greatly under his oversight," the *Pentecostal Evangel* noted. "Through camp meetings, fellowship meetings and conventions, he emphasized world missions with the result that many Kansas young people became foreign missionaries, and many others became pioneer preachers in the homeland."

As leader of national home missions, he directed the eight specific areas assigned to that area: new works, ministry to the deaf, foreign language groups, industrial chaplaincies, American Indian missions, Jewish evangelism, prison evangelism, and Alaska missions. His interest in Alaska soon resulted in more Assemblies of God churches in Alaska than churches of any other Protestant denomination.

In 1945 the Education and Home Missions Department was divided and a separate Home Missions Department with two divisions resulted: Church Extension and Special Ministries. Church Extension's main responsibility was starting new churches. This is still true. Today the New Church Evangelism Department under the Division of Home Missions has reaffirmed the establishment of new churches as a priority for the 1980s. Its goal is to see at least 300 new churches open each year during the decade.

Special Ministries included the Assemblies of God outreach in Alaska, ministries to ethnic groups, inner-city evangelism, work among the blind and deaf, and the various chaplaincies.

Among the earliest of these outreaches was the ministry to native Americans. It began without official national appointment of workers and was later integrated into the national program. In 1943 the Home Missions Department set up an American Indian Division to coordinate efforts among the many tribes scattered on hundreds of reservations.

A vital part of Assemblies of God ministry to Indians is the training of Indian workers. This is not the province of the Division of Home Missions alone. Indian training is done mainly through the American Indian Bible College founded in 1957 on the property of an Assemblies of God church in Phoenix, Arizona. It was known as All Tribes Bible School until 1966 when several districts and the national Home Missions Division assumed responsibility for it. Its curriculum includes both religious and technical programs.

Eastern Indian Bible School in North Carolina and Central Indian Bible College in South Dakota have been developed through their districts to make training available for native Americans.

Some of the ministries directed toward ethnic groups originate in the districts; others have a close relationship to programs developed in the Division of Home Missions. Home Missions has 22 missionaries nationally appointed to ministries among 12 foreign-language groups in the United States. The Special Ministries Department has about 300 appointed home missionaries serving ethnic and minority groups. Many local churches also reach out to ethnic populations that surround them.

The national office appoints leaders for 25 Jewish

churches and centers. It sponsors an annual national conference for Jewish believers called Ruach.

The Division of Home Missions coordinates ministries to the deaf, the blind, and the handicapped. The division sponsors braille literature and a tape library. Some course studies from the Berean College of the Assemblies of God are available on tape for the blind.

Work among the deaf, although officially placed under the national office in 1952, originated with individual workers in the 1920s. Tracts for the deaf and a newsletter called *The Cosigner* for workers among the deaf help make the Assemblies of God outreach to this group among the most organized of any evangelical effort.

Teen Challenge has won recognition for its ministry to drug-dependent young people. Born out of the vision of David Wilkerson, Teen Challenge has expanded from its original base in Brooklyn, New York, to include 100 ministries, 67 of which have residential programs. In its training courses, former drug addicts, alcoholics, and prostitutes receive instruction in their faith and learn to share it. Teen Challenge is active in schools, prisons, and on the streets of American cities in 33 states and Puerto Rico.

Throughout most of the denomination's history, Assemblies of God members have looked for ways to minister in prisons and other institutions. Lay volunteers added their efforts to those of local pastors in prison outreaches. During the 1950s, the denomination began in various ways to support a regular prison ministry. A special series of correspondence courses was developed for inmates.

Paul Markstrom, a pastor in Newburgh, New York, learned of the need for denominational assistance for chaplains in New York's prison system through a conversation with a Methodist chaplain. In August 1950, he

traveled to Springfield to share his burden for an organized prison outreach with the Fellowship's executive
leaders. He returned the next month to address the General Presbytery. As a result, Arvid Ohrnell, the first
Assemblies of God minister to have served as a state-
appointed prison chaplain, was invited to Springfield to
organize a denominational prison ministry.

Just hours before receiving the General Presbytery's
invitation, Orhnell had resigned from 16 years of service
in the prison at Walla Walla, Washington. Unknown to
anyone in Springfield, Ohrnell had already developed
plans for a denominational prison ministry. After accepting the new position, Ohrnell supervised the growth
of an effective outreach to prison inmates for more than
12 years. He suffered a fatal heart attack while visiting
the Louisiana State Penitentiary in 1963. Paul Markstrom, whose burden had helped shape the ministry,
assumed leadership.

In 1973 the chaplaincy area became a separate department under the Division of Home Missions. This
department assumed responsibility for the oversight of
institutional and military chaplains.

The denomination also appoints part- and full-time
industrial and hospital chaplains. The 1985 roster shows
60 correctional, 22 hospital, and 16 industrial Assemblies
of God chaplains.

Military ministries provide both literature to members
of the Armed Forces and liaison with chaplains in the
Army, Navy, Air Force, and Marines. The Assemblies
of God has more military chaplains (76) on active duty
than ever before. Several more are awaiting endorse-
ment. Six Veterans Administration chaplains serve in
veterans' hospitals. Retreats for military personnel offer
opportunities for fellowship and outreach. Annual retreats for the military and institutional chaplains help

keep them related more closely to the parent church body.

The Division of Home Missions coordinates ministries to a variety of peoples and needs. Together with ministries from other divisions that provide many kinds of support for its endeavors, Home Missions is an important part of the commitment of the Assemblies of God to evangelism and church growth.

6

The Tumultuous Forties

The Assemblies of God organized just before World War I. During that war, the Fellowship leaned toward pacifism. For example, E. S. Williams (general superintendent from 1929 to 1949) recalled that the baptism in the Holy Spirit had filled him with such love that he found it impossible to have a part in war.

E. N. Bell, on the other hand, wrote: "[The believer] is not a murderer when he obeys his country in executing just punishment on the criminal Hun." Both views existed side by side in the Fellowship, with pacifism probably reflecting the majority.

Several times during World War I, General Councils stated the Fellowship's loyalty to the government. Some members of the Executive Presbytery filed an unofficial resolution in favor of conscientious objection in Washington, D. C. The Fellowship also endorsed evangelistic outreaches among the soldiers.

The events of World War II drew a different response. In general, Americans went to war with less optimism. They fought, not "to make the world safe for democracy" or "to end all wars," but rather for human survival.

The bombing of Pearl Harbor united many Americans in a patriotic cause. "Freedom of religion . . . everywhere in the world" was one of the "four freedoms" Franklin Roosevelt set forth as goals. American Protestants, including many Pentecostals, sought to preserve democracy and religious liberty. Some chose conscientious objection and noncombatant service. Others fought. Some of the denomination's pioneers regretted the change in attitude; the patriotic enthusiasm with which Assemblies of God members went to war seemed to mean something in the heritage had been lost.

In fact, the patriotism had always been there, perhaps not so evident in the Assemblies of God as in some other Pentecostal groups. Religion and militant patriotism were fused in many people's minds. The result was wholehearted participation in all phases of the war: fighting, noncombatant service, employment in war-related industries.

Like other American women, some Assemblies of God women joined the work force. This fact became part of a broader trend redefining family relationships. Students left schools to help the war effort. Assemblies of God educators felt pressure to adjust their curricula to meet the higher academic standards necessary for transferring their credits to other schools. Accreditation became a matter that would fundamentally affect the training at all the endorsed schools.

As they had in World War I, Assemblies of God members recognized the evangelistic opportunities in World War II. The theme "Our Place in the Present World Crisis" was chosen for the General Council that met in Minneapolis in 1941.

Some had already begun to work among servicemen. The Council listened to their suggestions and adopted a resolution with a twofold aim. First, they committed themselves "to maintain spiritual watchcare over our boys in the Armed Service." Second, they decided to try "evangelization of army camps, naval bases, and Civilian Conservation Camps."

The carrying out of this plan was put in the hands of Myer Pearlman, an instructor at Central Bible Institute. After Pearlman's death in 1943, Fred Vogler, secretary of home missions, led the program until the Servicemen's Department was set up in 1944.

Some Assemblies of God ministers sought appointment as chaplains. They discovered strict requirements, including a 4-year college degree and a 3-year theological seminary degree. Few, if any, had that kind of training. In the war crisis, however, these requirements were occasionally waived. Experience in the ministry or other qualifications were accepted as substitutes for the formal training.

During the war, 34 Assemblies of God ministers left their churches to serve as military chaplains. About 76,000 Assemblies of God men served in the military; 1,093 were killed.

The work load of the Servicemen's Department dropped off rapidly after 1945. Its main responsibilities were among occupation forces in Europe and the Pacific. In 1946, its remaining ministries were placed under the Youth Department (then the Christ's Ambassador's Department).

In the long run, taking part in World War II brought into focus the potential of accredited college programs and seminary courses. For many years, the growing number of Assemblies of God chaplains had to pursue their academic training in non-Pentecostal schools. Their need for accredited degrees is an important part of the development of Assemblies of God sponsored seminary training.

It is easy to compare and contrast situations in the Assemblies of God before and after World War II. The close relationship between religion and culture comes into sharp focus.

During the 1920s and 1930s, Pentecostals were isolated from one another. Doctrinal and organizational differences separated them. In those years the American Pentecostal movement nourished independent, magnetic leaders. Some of them won wide followings. Some had denominational affiliations; others preferred independence; but all enjoyed interdenominational support.

Aimee Semple McPherson was among them. Dramatic and forceful, she captured the attention of the nation as she held vast healing and evangelistic services across the country.

Probably McPherson's most famous convert was Charles S. Price, an Englishman who came to the United States via Canada. Price had a law degree from Oxford University. He had pastored well-to-do Methodist and Congregational churches on the west coast before he was saved and Spirit-filled in McPherson's tent in 1922. He immediately became a healing evangelist himself.

Independent English Pentecostal Smith Wigglesworth also won widespread support. John Lake ministered physical healing in large services across the northwest. F. F. Bosworth continued his evangelistic campaigns and also became a pioneer radio evangelist. Raymond T. Richey, an Assemblies of God minister, held salvation-healing services in Texas that received wide press coverage.

By the end of World War II, all of these except Bosworth and Richey had died. During the 1940s, it became increasingly apparent that the Assemblies of God needed revival. Many of its members had never received the baptism in the Holy Spirit. Young people and new converts had never seen anyone healed.

Almost from the beginning of the Assemblies of God, some people had talked about "declension," a falling away. And some of them tended to live in the past,

measuring the Fellowship's spirituality by the spontaneity of the Azusa Street revival. They found it sadly wanting. Others sincerely sought to force uniformity in matters
that had been left to the individual. Disregarding these
"reformers," however, signs of apathy remained. The
need for a "new Pentecost" for these second and third
generations became apparent.

The Assemblies of God was not without prophetic
voices. Some were raised within the Fellowship; others,
like that of Charles Price, were raised without. Price
called the American Pentecostals of the 1940s to a clear
and balanced sense of God's purpose in their generation.

"For the experiences of yesterday we praise God," he
told them, but "in vain we pray for the revival of yesterday." "To sit down and agonize and plead for a restoration of the things which contributed to the growth
of the people of the Lord two or three decades ago is to
miss the Divine Purpose. . . . Yesterday we sang 'Show-
ers of Blessing,' but now we are waiting for the DEL-
UGE."

Price admonished his readers to prepare for a revival.
This included separation from the world. "We have gone
down to Egypt," he admitted, "perhaps not to dwell
completely there, but . . . to borrow a few horses and
take a little ride in some gaily painted chariot. . . . But
the voice of the Lord is speaking. . . . What a call from
the eternal heavens to those who are spiritually alive to
separate themselves from the world and the flesh. . . .
We have our choice; the issues are clear; the flesh must
be crucified."

Others shared his awareness of the need but responded with less balance and less confidence than Price.
During the late 1940s, the call to separation and new
spiritual experience was sounded within Canadian and
American Pentecostalism. The "new order of the latter

rain" became an attempt to revive the Pentecostal movement.

The "New Order of the Latter Rain"

The aims of "latter rain" leaders were basically those of restorationists. Like the Pentecostal movement in 1901, the latter rain had roots in an independent faith Bible school (in North Battleford, Saskatchewan). There, it was claimed, in mid-February 1948, God began to restore apostolic offices and practices to the church. This was the "latter rain" the prophet Joel had spoken of.

As latter rain teaching spread, it picked up different emphases. Its supporters were not agreed among themselves, except on several general themes. They tended to reject the organized Pentecostal movement as "dead" or "apostate." Miracles, spontaneity, and spiritual gifts had been withdrawn from Pentecostalism, they claimed, because it had compromised with the world and ignored important New Testament teaching.

Latter rain people tended to be extreme congregationalists. They opposed formal organization, except in the local church. They taught that the gifts of the Spirit should come through the laying on of hands. Some thought that through the laying on of hands and prophecy, each member of the congregation could find his special place in the body of Christ.

In some congregations, prophecy was given a place equal to Scripture—or above it. Alarmed, Assemblies of God leaders pointed out that some latter rain teachers had "launched out in the realm of spiritual guidance, and their beliefs of today may not be the beliefs of tomorrow."

Latter rain ministries also stressed their God-given authority to bring about deliverances from sinful habits, demons, diseases, phobias, mental bondage, and many other things. This authority stemmed from the gift of "the keys of the kingdom of heaven."

In North Battleford, and then in many other places—Detroit; St. Louis; Memphis; Beaumont, Texas; and Portland, Oregon—this teaching found support. Many of its advocates sincerely desired a new move of God. Feeling a lack of spiritual gifts and ministries, they responded to those who invited them to share in the "great restoration."

Besides the restoration of apostles, prophets, elders, and deacons, the North Battleford center noted the restoration of church discipline; the sacraments (including foot washing), with new revelations of their meaning; apostolic doctrine ("further unfolding" the mind of God); spiritual worship and singing; spiritual giving ("If they give one tenth, they are not giving in the Spirit. When they commence to give more than one tenth, they are getting out of the realm of the law. But when they give hilariously . . . then they are giving in the Spirit.").

The focus of the restoration was on Christ's second coming. In this emphasis, too, it seemed that Pentecostals were being recalled to their heritage. "All things must be restored before He shall come," they taught. "He will remain in the heavens until this restitution is complete."

The difference between these emphases and the doctrines of their Pentecostal heritage was too subtle for some Pentecostals to discern. They simply felt they were being recalled to a "deeper" spiritual experience and the supernatural element in worship. Many latter rain centers emphasized separation and decried the worldliness and formalism that, they charged, had crept into Pentecostalism. All of them agreed that latter rain believers were in revival and the Pentecostal movement as a whole was "woefully backslidden."

Several Pentecostal groups were affected by this teaching. In the Assemblies of God, district and national periodicals tried to point out the errors and extremes of the teaching without starting outright controversy. In the end, the Assemblies of God lost few ministers and churches. The most vigorous congregation to withdraw was Bethesda Tabernacle in Detroit, pastored by Myrtle Beall. The most prominent individual linked for a time with latter rain was Stanley Frodsham, editor of the *Pentecostal Evangel,* who went with the movement for a time after his resignation in 1949.

The Healing Revival

The "new order of the latter rain" attracted only a small following, primarily among Pentecostals. Another revival, happening at the same time, had more far-reaching significance for American religion. The years right after the war saw the birth of organized healing revivalism. It popularized the Pentecostal message and later would be one source of the charismatic movement's vitality.

The promoter of healing revivalism was an Assemblies of God minister, Gordon Lindsay. Lindsay looked upon the postwar healing revival as the "breakthrough" Charles Price had foreseen.

From the beginning, Assemblies of God pastors and teachers had stressed the doctrine of divine healing. Like their teachers, A. B. Simpson, A. J. Gordon, and J. A. Dowie, they felt that healing was in the Atonement for all believers. Some, like Lilian Yeomans, wrote regularly for the Fellowship's publications on the subject of healing. Others were known for praying for the sick. Reports of healings were common in Pentecostal papers.

During the depression years, the scarcity of money

limited the ministries of well-known healing evangelists. Evidence suggests that healings (at least of the dramatic type) hardly happened in some local congregations. Some people were worried that the next generation of Pentecostals would have only a knowledge of the doctrine of healing, not an experience.

The new emphasis on healing after World War II began with William Branham, a Baptist who discovered the gift of healing and then found a welcome among Oneness Pentecostals. Soon afterwards, he met Gordon Lindsay; through him he gained acceptance among some Assemblies of God people. Branham drew thousands of followers to his meetings, where, many agreed, various spiritual gifts operated.

Before long, Oral Roberts' meetings drew public attention and other healing evangelists arose. Many of them held credentials with the Assemblies of God.

Gordon Lindsay served most of the healing revivalists as promoter. His magazine and organization, both known as *The Voice of Healing*, announced campaign schedules, held conventions, and tried to keep harmony among the leaders. As the movement grew, however, Lindsay found it impossible to enforce standards of practice or confirm claims of miracles.

By the early 1950s concern about the methods and characters of several of the well-known evangelists surfaced. Assemblies of God leaders did not quarrel with the evangelists over the doctrine of healing itself. Rather, they were worried about some who exploited the ministry for profit or discredited the Assemblies of God (and the entire Pentecostal movement) by their conduct.

Another problem developed as some healing evangelists began to raise funds for missions. Assemblies of God missionaries agreed with others who felt that the distribution of funds for "native evangelism" encouraged a "loaves and fishes" following. It also ran against the principle of founding churches that supported themselves.

As early as 1949, the General Council began to deal with matters surrounding the healing revival. The *Pentecostal Evangel* neither carried reports of the healing campaigns nor published testimonies of healings occurring in them. It continued to report healings in local congregations that were endorsed by credentialed pastors.

In the next several years, many of the revivalists withdrew from the Assemblies of God. The denomination set up a committee to study all aspects of the situation. General Superintendent Ralph M. Riggs wrote an open letter to the Fellowship entitled "The Doctrine of Divine Healing Is Being Wounded in the House of Its Friends."

The early energy generated by the healing revival began to weaken in the mid-1950s. *The Voice of Healing* listed fewer and fewer cooperating evangelists as more and more of them chose independence.

In the Assemblies of God, the healing revival renewed interest in the subject of healing. Where the doctrine had been neglected, it was reemphasized. The yearning to "see what we believe" was met, not only in the mass campaigns but also in local congregations. In the long run, as one leader saw it, the most effective proclamation of healing came from local pulpits where pastors consistently ministered a Biblical message and the congregation faithfully prayed for the sick. True divine healing, some felt, included spiritual discipline, which healing revivalists too often neglected.

Both the "new order of the latter rain" and the salvation-healing revival won followers in Assemblies of God ranks. Their emphases seemed to meet certain needs. In one sense, these movements can be understood as part of a reaction to increasing "orderliness" in Pentecostal worship. Both of them promoted a degree of antidenominationalism aimed at the Assemblies of God and other Pentecostal fellowships. Pentecostal denominations, in turn, saw in such ranks signs of "the confusion which was so prevalent during the early [unorganized] days of the Pentecostal movement." The controversy over organization, one of the oldest in the Pentecostal movement, has persisted throughout its history.

Evangelist Charles Price had called the 1940s a "momentous hour" and had prophesied a new "move" of God. Both the new order of the latter rain and the healing revival were presented as the "deluge" God had promised. But neither was accepted as such by the Assemblies of God, even though both expressed a longing for reality that was shared throughout the Fellowship.

Yet, in another sense, in the 1940s the Assemblies of God *was* experiencing "momentous" changes. It moved from isolation into involvement with the broader American religious scene.

7

The Evangelical Community

During the 1940s, the Assemblies of God began to cooperate in evangelical efforts outside the Fellowship. It also identified with other Pentecostals at home and abroad. These events convinced some within the Assemblies of God that they were living in a momentous hour. As the denomination moved from isolation into a role of evangelical and Pentecostal leadership, it both caused change and underwent change.

Before World War II, the Assemblies of God and other American Pentecostal groups developed separately. Each had its form of church order, its doctrinal emphases, and its gifted leaders. Since divisions over doctrines like sanctification and the Trinity (before 1918), American Pentecostal bodies had not maintained much contact among themselves.

This situation cannot be blamed on doctrinal differences alone. Some of the groups sprang up with limited outside Pentecostal influence and never tried to go beyond where they originated. At the same time, their own local influence met with persecution. The poverty of some Pentecostal groups also limited their reaching out to sister groups; mere survival took all their attention and resources. What's more, expectations of Christ's soon return overshadowed such secondary matters as relationships with other groups, Pentecostal or not.

On top of this, Pentecostalism itself was rejected by those whose beliefs otherwise seemed so similar to those Christians who had accepted it. Ignored by liberals, Pentecostals were outspokenly opposed by their conservative brethren.

Opposition to Pentecostalism

Holiness groups called the Pentecostal doctrine of Spirit baptism "third blessing heresy." Alma White, founder and leader of the Pillar of Fire (a holiness group with a sizable following in Colorado and New Jersey), wrote a book titled *Demons and Tongues* in which she argued that Pentecostal tongues were demon inspired. *Tongues Movement Satanic* by W. B. Godby reached the same conclusions. Some holiness groups stopped using the term *Pentecostal* (which had been common among them) and played down the similarities between their heritage and Pentecostalism's.

American fundamentalism became a self-conscious movement in the years just before Pentecostalism. Its adherents opposed American Protestantism's growing theological liberalism. Many of them were premillennialists. The heritage of the Assemblies of God had been influenced by their views. Fundamentalists held to the verbal inspiration of Scripture. After 1909, most of them eagerly read the *Scofield Reference Bible* (which the *Pentecostal Evangel* often promoted).

Some of the early fundamentalists had taught divine healing and faith living. R. A. Torrey had encouraged all Christian workers to seek the baptism in the Holy Spirit. A. T. Pierson had improved their understanding of their evangelistic obligations. The Assemblies of God was deeply indebted to these men. Through the pages of the *Evangel*, their books were often recommended to the constituency.

Nevertheless, as holiness advocates had done, fundamentalists separated themselves from Pentecostals (as well as from holiness groups) by 1914. Those fundamentalists who shared most fully in the Pentecostal heritage generally rejected the concept of a "uniform Biblical evidence" of Spirit baptism. They also pointed to the confusion and extremes that sometimes marked early Pentecostalism as evidence that the Movement was not "of God."

Other fundamentalists fully accepted Scofield's dispensationalism and believed Spirit baptism was for another dispensation: the time of the Early Church. Some fundamentalists were embarrassed by the emotionalism and disorder they saw in Pentecostalism. At the same time, they felt they had to say something about the major theological issues of the day as part of their effort to stop modernism. In 1910 the launching of a series of 12 small books called *The Fundamentals* began a new phase in the history of fundamentalism.

This careful definition of the fundamentals of the faith made the doctrinal mix of Pentecostalism look appalling. Pentecostal objections (like those in the Assemblies of God) to restrictive doctrinal statements troubled fundamentalists. And they believed some of the unfavorable rumors about Pentecostal leaders and practices. As a result, in the fundamentalists' efforts to prove their orthodoxy, they generally considered Pentecostal and holiness followers hindrances.

The fundamentalists had a point. The Assemblies of God itself had begun because some Pentecostals had similar concerns about their own Movement. But outsiders generally did not notice the careful distinctions many Pentecostals made between authentic and counterfeit spiritual manifestations. These critics chose instead to discredit the whole Movement because of the abuses in some of its less ordered segments.

The fundamentalists thought of themselves as the guardians of Biblical religion. It is hardly surprising that they did not welcome the help of Pentecostals. Yet the Assemblies of God following was certainly fundamentalist in many ways. They committed themselves to the verbal inspiration of Scripture and to crucial doctrines like the Virgin Birth, the substitutionary Atonement, and the physical Resurrection. "We are fundamentalist to a man," the *Pentecostal Evangel* proclaimed.

Assemblies of God members sympathized with fundamentalists in their struggles during the 1920s to prevent the teaching of evolution in public schools and to expose modernism in the denominations. But they were not welcome to formally take part in the fundamentalist cause.

The National Association of Evangelicals

By 1940, fundamentalism was badly fragmented. Concerned evangelicals noticed that fundamentalists opposed one another as strongly as they did liberal Protestants. Examining midcentury fundamentalism, some evangelicals were troubled by its negative way of exposing error. Carl Henry spoke for a growing group when he claimed: "Rededication to positive and triumphant preaching is the evangelical pulpit's great need."

Henry thought that evangelicalism was "overdenominationalized" and called for a new emphasis "on the unity of the body [of Christ]." Unfortunately, the concept of unity was generally linked with the broad membership of the growing liberal Christian movement. Throughout the 1940s, ecumenical efforts went forward until they formed the World Council of Churches at Amsterdam in 1948.

On the American scene, the Federal Council of Churches, formed in 1908, spoke more and more as if it represented all American Protestants. Its doctrinal basis was a simple affirmation of "the essential oneness of the Christian Churches of America, in Jesus Christ as their Lord and Saviour." But from its beginnings, the FCC had supported liberal social causes. Conservative evangelicals resented the thought that the Federal Council represented American Protestants.

In this disarray, during the early 1940s, two efforts were begun to unite conservative evangelicals. One had as its organizing principle attacking the Federal Council of Churches. This organization, the American Council of Christian Churches, led by Carl McIntire, originated with two small separatist, fundamentalist groups. It drew up a constitution, elected officers, and then invited others to join.

Many were troubled by the American Council's negative basis for united action. Some also thought that to organize successfully all potential members ought to be involved in the organizing effort at the outset. These people, led by such New England evangelicals as Harold J. Ockenga and J. Elwin Wright, called a meeting of evangelical leaders in St. Louis in 1942. They invited the Assemblies of God to participate. Other Pentecostal and holiness groups were also represented.

The Assemblies of God delegation included General Superintendent Ernest Williams, General Secretary J. R. Flower, and Missionary Secretary Noel Perkin, as well as Southern Missouri District Superintendent Ralph M. Riggs. The new group that was formed was called the National Association of Evangelicals (NAE). It called on evangelicals to find strength in unity. "The forces of unrighteousness have so laid siege," its leaders warned, "that we must be united in spirit and strategy."

Throughout the next year, churches and denominations joined the association. Assemblies of God pastors took part in local association gatherings around the country. General Secretary Flower served on several committees that drew up the policies of the NAE; his colleagues respected his counsel. The 1943 General Council voted to affiliate the Assemblies of God with the NAE.

For the first time, Pentecostals had been asked to work with other evangelicals. The Assemblies of God had been welcomed into a broader evangelical fellowship than it had ever known.

The NAE not only brought the Assemblies of God into the neoevangelical community, but also brought Pentecostals and holiness denominations into fellowship with each other. Some of the old uncertainties about one another had already been overcome, but contact through the NAE opened discussion that helped to heal old wounds.

In the NAE, American Pentecostals worked together in new ways. They found that they were more alike than different.

For the first few years, some fundamentalists expressed reservations about Pentecostal membership. The neoevangelical leaders, however, had a different philosophy of their task than did their more radically fundamentalist advisors. Reports in some publications—secular, liberal Protestant, and fundamentalist—belittled the NAE because it included holiness and Pentecostal groups. General Secretary Flower often urged the president of the NAE, Harold Ockenga, to avoid difficulty by playing down Pentecostal participation in the organization.

President Ockenga was firm, however. "If there is to be any revival in our age, it must come through the emphasis upon the Holy Ghost," he wrote to Flower.

"You may be sure that . . . we shall attempt to follow the leadings of the Holy Spirit. He shall be given His proper place in the church. . . . I have no desire to push into the background the Pentecostals, the Nazarenes, the Free Methodists or any others who are so-called holiness groups. I am sure that without holiness, no man shall see the Lord."

In contrast to the previous decades of arguing among evangelicals, neoevangelicals stressed a "positive proclamation" of evangelical beliefs. And it soon became clear that they had fully accepted the Assemblies of God as an evangelical denomination. From the beginning, NAE leaders sought the participation of members and leaders of the Assemblies of God. Thomas F. Zimmerman attended the 1943 St. Louis meeting as an unofficial observer. He would serve as president of the NAE during his first years as general superintendent of the Assemblies of God (1960-1962) and afterwards serve on its executive committee.

But Flower saw that more was at stake than simply an acceptance of denominations like the Assemblies of God as evangelicals. "If the NAE serves no other purpose than to provide a medium to better understanding among the holiness and Pentecostal people, it shall have rendered a great service," he wrote in 1943.

Among the first concerns of the NAE itself was the fear that the Federal Council of Churches would exclude evangelicals from broadcasting the gospel. The activities of some independent Pentecostal and fundamentalist radio preachers had drawn charges of religious racketeering. So the Federal Council, it seemed to evangelicals, had decided to convince the networks that it represented mainstream Protestantism.

Evangelical broadcasters were specially invited to attend the second NAE convention, held in Columbus,

Ohio, in April 1944. The 150 who responded organized the National Religious Broadcasters (NRB) on April 14 to affirm the right of evangelicals to air time. Its activities over the next 2 years reversed the situation that had seemed to threaten their right to broadcast.

Thomas F. Zimmerman was a member of this organization's original executive committee. He served as its president, 1954-1956, and remains a member of the executive committee. Others in Assemblies of God broadcasting have also worked at various levels of the NRB.

The NAE has other agencies that have been important to the Assemblies of God. The denomination has benefited especially from participation in both the National Sunday School Association and the Evangelical Foreign Missions Association.

The World Pentecostal Conference

As the Assemblies of God accepted the invitation of evangelicals to united action, Pentecostals in other countries were doing the same. Growing acceptance of them was occurring not only because evangelicals had changed but also, as Donald Gee noted, because Pentecostals were finally "ready to drop their sometime too ready criticism of the denominational churches."

During the late 1930s, several Pentecostals had begun to explore the possibilities of broader Pentecostal fellowship. Two who became important in this effort were Donald Gee, a leader in the British Assemblies of God, and David du Plessis, of the South African Apostolic Faith Mission. (Du Plessis later affiliated with the American Assemblies of God when he became pastor of one of their churches in Connecticut.) Assemblies of God leaders expressed interest in taking part in an international Pentecostal gathering.

The worsening world political situation made such a meeting impractical at the time. However, in June 1939 European Pentecostals from 20 different countries attended a week-long conference in Stockholm. After World War II, memories of that meeting prompted plans for another. This time, however, attendance would not be only European.

The Assemblies of God, and some other Pentecostal groups, were engaged in relief work among the dispossessed in Europe. The Americans wanted to help this effort and make it more effective. They also longed to encourage the suffering Pentecostal believers in Europe. Together, the leaders hoped, representatives of a wide spectrum of the Pentecostal movement could address urgent needs and understand their role in the new tensions of the postwar years.

The first World Pentecostal Conference met in Zurich, Switzerland, in May 1947. Among the vice chairmen was Assemblies of God General Superintendent Ernest S. Williams. Serious divisions quickly became apparent. All agreed that relief work was urgent. But, as Donald Gee recalled, some delegates had come for "spiritual discussions" and others for "practical purposes."

In addition, some opposed putting together any permanent organization. Scandinavian Pentecostals, in particular, accepted only the authority of the local congregation. The fear that local authority might be given up to a central agency resulted in long and difficult discussion. For a time, this endangered the attempt to promote worldwide fellowship.

Out of the first world conference came a magazine to carry the news of the worldwide Pentecostal movement. Donald Gee accepted its editing responsibilities. The paper was known as *Pentecost* (now *World Pentecost*).

In spite of difficulties, the first World Pentecostal Conference had deep meaning for Pentecostalism. As Donald Gee said, "It marked the definite self-consciousness of the movement as a recognizable worldwide entity. . . . It marked the culmination of a process that had begun nearly forty years before, when denominational opposition compelled the formation of . . . Pentecostal assemblies all over the land. Gradually, imperceptibly, but inevitably the original vision of a Pentecostal REVIVAL that should inspire and quicken the existing denominations faded." In other words, the World Pentecostal Conference displayed "a fully-developed denominational complex."

Gee noted that, in the future, Pentecostalism would influence other groups as "one sect among many." The Pentecostal revival had spawned new denominations. It had not survived as a "force."

Yet Gee was optimistic. The Movement had institutionalized the revival and, to a degree, had directed its influence. However, its significance for people continued. "It is individuals who backslide—not Movements," he noted. "It is individuals who retain the Anointing—not Movements. . . . Membership of the true Pentecostal Movement . . . is not membership of any sect or even of any Pentecostal church . . . [but] being filled with the Holy Spirit 'as at the beginning' and continuing in the fulness. . . . The continuance of the Movement as a revival will not depend upon . . . busy organizing of all kinds of activity. . . . Always, and ultimately—IT ALL DEPENDS UPON ME."

So the desire for World Pentecostal Conferences survived the difficulties of the first meeting, and international gatherings have been held every 3 years since 1949. The Assemblies of God has consistently sought to maintain the early idea of a cooperative fellowship, and its leaders have gained respect in the worldwide Movement. General Superintendent Zimmerman has chaired the Advisory Committee for the Pentecostal World conferences since 1973.

Closer contact with other Pentecostals has enriched the Assemblies of God. Awareness of their participation in a worldwide Movement has helped Assemblies of God people recognize anew that the "unity of the Spirit" goes beyond denominational organization. This has helped to discourage a separatism that divides and to encourage the recognition of a basis for fellowship.

The Pentecostal Fellowship of North America

As some American Pentecostals came together, first as evangelicals in the NAE, then as part of an international movement in the World Pentecostal Conferences, they discovered the benefits of cooperative fellowship. They decided to try to bring together the American Pentecostal denominations.

European Pentecostals encouraged this effort. In the 1947 World Pentecostal Conference, Americans had tried to resolve the differences of their European brethren. The Europeans had pointed out that American Pentecostals remained equally divided. In Paris in 1949, as everyone moved toward a basis for broad, nonrestrictive, worldwide fellowship, European leaders challenged Americans to do the same at home.

The Americans had held a preliminary meeting in conjunction with the NAE convention in 1948. But not all American Pentecostals belonged to the NAE. The Church of God in Christ, largely black in membership, did not. Neither did some of the less centrally organized groups. Some Pentecostals were against associating with non-

Pentecostal evangelicals. They felt it would compromise their Pentecostal testimony.

Some of these groups also rejected the World Pentecostal Conferences on similar grounds. They maintained that only their interpretation of Pentecostalism was correct. They separated themselves from all Pentecostals who differed with them, coming to consider many of them apostate.

Such groups shared the heritage of the Assemblies of God but did not understand it in the same way. Their influence in the American religious culture and in the worldwide Pentecostal community has been severely limited by their exclusivism.

Those Pentecostals who recognized their own evangelical roots and who believed that fellowship did not mean compromise began work to bring together the various American Pentecostal groups. In Chicago, leaders of eight Pentecostal denominations met. J. R. Flower was chosen temporary secretary of their committee and served with a chairman from the Church of God (Cleveland, Tennessee).

At a second meeting with representatives from 12 denominations, Flower was appointed chairman of a committee to draw up a constitution. It would be proposed to a convention scheduled for October in Des Moines, Iowa. Out of this the Pentecostal Fellowship of North America (PFNA) was created and Canadian participation was invited.

In 1949, by formal action of the General Council, the Assemblies of God applied for membership in the PFNA. Twenty-four Pentecostal denominations today make up the membership. The Assemblies of God continues to be the largest affiliated group. The smaller groups have contributed important leadership. The Assemblies of God has been well represented by J. R. Flower, Gayle F. Lewis, G. Raymond Carlson, and Thomas Zimmerman.

The PFNA has brought American and Canadian Pentecostal leaders together. It has been less successful in cultivating fellowship among Pentecostals at the local level.

The goals of the new fellowship included coordination of evangelistic efforts and a show of "the essential unity of Spirit-baptized believers." It agreed from the outset that each group would keep its "every freedom." Its doctrinal statement excluded Oneness Pentecostals from membership.

The Charismatic Movement

During the 1940s, then, the Assemblies of God went through significant changes. Internally, it looked at new issues raised during World War II. In the religious community, it gained some acceptance among those who had rejected it a generation earlier. New avenues of communication were opened among Pentecostals around the world.

All this happened within a larger religious culture that was also concentrating on unity. Ecumenical efforts grew, especially among liberal Protestants.

Meanwhile, the healing revivalists were taking the "full gospel" to many people who had never attended a Pentecostal service. Generally, their revival campaigns were not restricted to any particular audience, and some in their audiences were stirred to take the emphasis on the Holy Spirit and spiritual gifts into their own denominations.

One of the agencies that came out of the healing revival was the Full Gospel Business Men's Fellowship, International. Its aim was to promote Pentecostal fellowship across denominational lines. It soon became part of the charismatic renewal, offering a setting outside the church in which Pentecostal teaching and worship could flourish.

Besides the healing revival, the charismatic movement had other origins. During the 1950s, well-known liberal Protestants had begun to notice Pentecostals. Henry Pitney van Dusen of New York's Union Theological Seminary said Pentecostalism was a "third force" in Christendom and called his fellow liberals to take note of its advances as it focused on the Holy Spirit.

In 1951, David du Plessis, an Assemblies of God minister, visited the leaders of the World Council of Churches in New York City and shared the Pentecostal message with them. No one was more surprised than du Plessis at the interest he found. He was invited to take part in ecumenical gatherings and won the friendship of such men as John Mackay, president of Princeton Theological Seminary, and Willem Visser 't Hooft, general secretary of the World Council of Churches.

In his dealings with these liberal Protestants, du Plessis encouraged them to accept a Pentecostal encounter with the Holy Spirit. He told them to stay in their churches, and he refused to pass sentence on their theology. This caused concern in the Assemblies of God and other Pentecostal groups.

The experience of Dennis Bennett, an Episcopalian priest in Van Nuys, California, also helped popularize the experience of Spirit baptism in mainstream denominations. Bennett and others in his congregation received the baptism in the Holy Spirit late in 1959. News of the resulting turmoil in the dioceses appeared in both *Time* and *Newsweek*. Pentecostal teaching and worship spread in other churches on the west coast and then across the country.

During the 1960s, du Plessis also became identified with Catholic Pentecostalism. The charismatic movement in the Catholic Church had at its origin an Assemblies of God influence. In 1966, several lay Catholic faculty members at Duquesne University in Pittsburgh read David Wilkerson's *The Cross and the Switchblade*. This account of his Teen Challenge ministry included a Pentecostal interpretation of the supernatural occurrences.

After reading other books about the charismatic renewal in Protestant denominations, these men began to fellowship with local charismatic Christians. Catholic neo-Pentecostalism (or charismatic renewal), born at Duquesne, energized renewals at Notre Dame and other places. It attracted tens of thousands of followers in the next decade.

For the Assemblies of God and other Pentecostal denominations, the charismatic movement raised some troubling questions. While classical (or traditional) Pentecostals insisted that they welcomed any genuine outpouring of the Holy Spirit, they wondered how such renewal could come without acceptance of the evangelical faith. They were concerned over the continuation of practices they had long rejected as incompatible with the indwelling Holy Spirit. If the Spirit "led into all truth," why did neo-Pentecostals not see the truth the way classical Pentecostals did?

Some Pentecostals—like du Plessis—answered by saying that unity could be found in experience rather than in doctrine and readily embraced the neo-Pentecostal renewal. Because he could not conscientiously follow the Executive Presbytery's guidelines regarding ministry in the World Council of Churches, du Plessis terminated his credentials with the Assemblies of God in 1962.

Other teaching that arose in the charismatic movement also troubled classical Pentecostals. Some charismatics denied that speaking in tongues was the "uniform initial evidence" of Spirit baptism. And most of them rejected the life-style that had historically been a part of classical Pentecostalism.

On the local level, classical and new Pentecostals were engaged in a great deal of exchange. Congregations of classical Pentecostals were renewed through contacts with enthusiastic charismatic Christians. Charismatic worship styles brought refreshing spontaneity and informality to some formal Pentecostal churches.

In 1972, leaders of the Assemblies of God affirmed their desire to identify the Fellowship with "what God is doing in the world today." "The winds of the Spirit are blowing freely outside the normally recognized Pentecostal bodies," they acknowledged. "The Assemblies of God does not place approval on that which is manifestly not scriptural in doctrine or conduct, but neither do we categorically condemn everything that does not totally . . . conform to our standards. It is important to find our way on a scriptural path, avoiding extremes of an ecumenism that compromises scriptural principles and an exclusivism that excludes true Christianity."

In 1980, David du Plessis (who had remained a member of an Assemblies of God congregation) again became a credentialed Assemblies of God minister. More recently, by sponsoring Conferences on the Holy Spirit in Springfield, Missouri, in 1982 and 1984, the Assemblies of God has sought to provide an interdenominational setting in which all who want to exalt the Holy Spirit can study and worship together.

The events of the 1940s, then, both showed the full-fledged denominationalism of the Assemblies of God and helped it begin to move beyond this denominational awareness. The Assemblies of God readily admitted its basic unity with fellow evangelicals. In the 1950s, however, a new outpouring of the Holy Spirit revealed the need to affirm the unity of all who truly experience the Holy Spirit.

This did not mean, however, that either the evangelical message or its associated life-style was seen as less important. The Assemblies of God continues to stand for the historic fundamentals of the evangelical faith. It continues to affirm a classical Pentecostal understanding of the baptism in the Holy Spirit. And it still seeks to encourage outward as well as inward separation from the world.

Its ability to identify on appropriate occasions with "what God is doing" throughout the world without compromising its distinctive testimony has enabled it to extend its influence in the American religious culture.

8

The Ministry to Youth

During the period surrounding World War II, the General Council of the Assemblies of God developed significant new programs. Missions leaders planned to meet postwar needs. Auxiliary programs supporting evangelistic outreach were authorized in other departments. As returning GIs flocked to America's campuses and as higher education became more common, the Assemblies of God sponsored a campus outreach. Since then, programs with a youth emphasis have been developed. Through them, the Movement's youth, from preschoolers through college-age, have become an important part of Assemblies of God ministries.

Through its programs for youth, the denomination has shown its commitment to discipling its future leaders.

The Youth Department

During the 1940s, the national Youth Department was set up by the Assemblies of God. For many years, the Movement's commitment to youth ministries had been apparent. At an early stage, this was shown by the creation of national and regional Bible institutes to offer young men and women training for Christian service.

Most leaders were convinced that young people were the Movement's most valuable resource. Their prayer was that each generation would receive its own Pentecost and catch the vision for world evangelization. So they considered programs through which youth could grow spiritually as well as contribute to the Movement.

California pastors devised the earliest systematic youth program in the Fellowship. In 1925, under the leadership of Wesley R. Steelberg, churches in the Oakland and Stockton areas organized Pentecostal youth rallies using the name Pentecostal Ambassadors for Christ. A. G. Osterberg, then a pastor in Fresno, held similar gatherings. He called the participants Christian Crusaders. A Los Angeles youth pastor, Carl Hatch, chose the name Christ's Ambassadors (CAs) for the youth group in his church. This name (based on 2 Corinthians 5:20) captured the attention of youth leaders across the nation and was widely adopted to refer to the Fellowship's youth programs.

The 1927 General Council showed this growing awareness of the need for a youth program by appointing a committee to study the role of youth in the Fellowship. Meanwhile, in the districts, work among youth continued to gain grass roots support.

The Southern California District began to publish *The Christ's Ambassadors Herald*; by the early 1930s, it had a national readership. In 1937, headquarters accepted the recommendation of the youth committee that the paper be nationally sponsored. The next year the *CA Herald*, edited by Robert Cunningham, became a Fellowship publication.

Early in the 1940s, the denomination sponsored several national Christ's Ambassadors conferences. As a result of them, youth leaders asked for a national youth office. The 1943 General Council responded by authorizing the CA Department. Ralph Harris, a Michigan pastor active in district CA affairs, became its first director.

Since the opening of the national department, a variety of significant outreaches have been organized to channel the energies and talents of Assemblies of God youth. Today the CA Department is known as the Youth Department.

Although the Youth Department oversees most youth programs, some are the responsibility of other departments. Together they continue to help accomplish the denomination's purpose. At the same time, by serving its youth and making a place for them to serve, the Assemblies of God helps extend its purpose and vision from one generation to the next.

Speed-the-Light

Ralph Harris devised Speed-the-Light (STL) in response to Noel Perkin's goals for missions in the postwar years. Harris proposed that the Fellowship's youth raise funds for specific missionary needs. At the National Youth Conference in 1944, the program was launched with a goal of $1 from each young person. The anticipated result was $100,000.

The idea was readily accepted and served the double purpose of aiding foreign missions and directing the energies of Assemblies of God young people into worthwhile activities. STL's potential became apparent right away. Modern transportation and new equipment were necessary for the advance of missions, especially at the end of World War II.

The purchase of a small airplane for use in Liberia—where the lack of roads made air or water travel necessary—showed how sound and timely the idea of STL was. Appeals came from missionaries everywhere. Some needed boats; others wanted trucks, jeeps, or bicycles. During the first year, 71 vehicles were purchased.

Speed-the-Light next supplied money to buy a large surplus airplane from the Army. The plane was named *The Ambassador*. Later, *The Ambassador II* was added. These planes helped Assemblies of God missionaries avoid the difficulty of overseas travel right after the war. From 1947 until the service was discontinued in 1951, the planes flew missionaries and equipment around the world. Eventually *The Ambassador II* was sold for what it originally cost, and the money was put back into Speed-the-Light.

Before long, requests for other kinds of equipment were being processed: printing presses, broadcasting equipment, public-address systems, copy machines. In this way the type of equipment supplied to missionaries by Assemblies of God youth was broadened. Speed-the-Light money also paid for the repair and maintenance of the equipment it purchased.

In some cases, STL equipment made it possible for missionaries to go where they could not go before. A motorboat, for example, took missionaries to unreached Indians of South America. A Speed-the-Light mule carried Leonard and Ada Bolton over trails vehicles could not pass, allowing them to reach the Lisu in southwest China.

Thousands of missionaries tell how their work on the field was improved by Speed-the-Light. Some who served in the years before Speed-the-Light went from ox carts, water buffalo, and bicycles to jeeps, station wagons, and motorboats. However, it was not the comfort and convenience that meant so much to them—it was the improved ability to spread the gospel.

Sixty to eighty percent of the missionary's ministry used STL equipment, according to a survey at one point.

Although Speed-the-Light began by helping foreign missions, it now helps home missions as well. It supports the auxiliary needs of personnel in Teen Challenge, prison ministries, ethnic outreaches, and efforts among the handicapped.

Since 1944, total Speed-the-Light giving has topped $40 million. In recent years, inflation, taxes, and import fees have greatly increased the cost and delivery of STL items. Today there are more missionaries than ever before, and the demands on Speed-the-Light are greater. The rapid advance of technology also makes it necessary to update equipment often. Many approved projects wait for funding. Speed-the-Light has given invaluable support to evangelistic outreach. It has also given significant purpose to several generations of Assemblies of God young people who made themselves a force in missions.

College Ministry

The Assemblies of God outreach to America's campuses grew out of a challenge by J. Robert Ashcroft, speaking to the National Sunday School Convention in Springfield, Missouri, in 1947. He encouraged the Fellowship to develop ministry to Assemblies of God students in secular colleges.

Members of the CA Department liked the idea. They began an informal newsletter, "College Fellowship Bulletin," which they sent to Assemblies of God young people attending nonchurch schools. At the time, the Movement's schools offered neither liberal arts programs nor accredited Bible degrees; with the number of American college students rapidly going up, the potential for college ministry seemed limitless.

However, the department had no resources to do more than the newsletter. Issued free, it was published somewhat irregularly because the people who put it together had to take time from other assignments. By 1951, over 300 names were on its mailing list.

Meanwhile, J. Calvin Holsinger, a Pennsylvania native with a degree in history from Pittsburgh University, had come to Springfield for ministerial training at Central Bible Institute. After finishing his studies, he was invited to teach history at CBI. He also taught Sunday school at Springfield's Central Assembly of God.

In both of these teaching situations, Holsinger stressed campus ministry. Gradually, local pastors as well as interested students came to share his excitement about the potential of a Pentecostal campus effort. Springfield pastors asked Holsinger to handle an outreach to their students in local colleges. At about the same time, national CA Department representatives asked him to work part-time and to help in the development of a national program for campus ministries.

Holsinger accepted both challenges. He became editor of the quarterly paper, which had been renamed *Campus Ambassador*, and began regular ministry on nearby campuses. Because of both local and national interest, Holsinger was able to use local groups to test ideas and methods while devising guidelines for a national ministry.

The circulation of *Campus Ambassador* rose rapidly. It included articles on doctrine and practical Christian living as well as denominational news. By 1958, nineteen hundred were on the mailing list.

Holsinger also had the responsibility of coming up with a name for the ministry. To please both college students and the general constituency in the days when few Assemblies of God members had any experience on secular campuses was a challenge. Holsinger decided to make it easy for the membership to identify the campus ministry with the Christ's Ambassadors program: He chose as a name Chi Alpha, the Greek letters for CA.

College ministries expanded rapidly. By 1962, when

the first full-time position was created in the college section of the CA Department, the circulation of *Campus Ambassador* approached 4,000 and 33 Chi Alpha chapters were registered with the national office.

During the 1970s, the national Chi Alpha office added student training conferences, campus ministers' seminars, and a training course for new campus ministers. In 1977, a fourfold philosophy of ministry (worship, fellowship, discipleship, witness) was adopted.

In the late 1970s, a growing interest in high school campus ministry resulted in the development of Youth Alive. At first this was supervised by those responsible for Chi Alpha. Then, in 1979, they were separated and a high school ministry specialist's position was created. Youth Alive now reaches out to some 700 junior and senior high schools.

Currently over 110 Chi Alpha groups in the United States have chartered; they are directed by 135 full-time and part-time campus ministers.

America's college campuses continue to challenge concerned evangelicals. Less than 5 percent of the 12 million students on American campuses identify with any evangelical campus ministry; about 4,000 participate in Chi Alpha. Although Assemblies of God efforts have seen impressive growth, they have only begun to address the need.

Ambassadors in Mission

In 1966, the Christ's Ambassadors Department launched a program of missions outreach. Known as Ambassadors in Mission (AIM), the program seeks to spread the gospel using short-term missions teams working with local churches and missionaries.

Young people between the ages of 16 and 29 raise their own funds and minister at selected sites. Their ministry includes many methods: door-to-door witnessing, street evangelism, drama, song, puppetry, literature distribution. The immediate goals may be outreach at a major sports event or the planting of a new church. The ultimate goal is to help local Christians "preach the gospel to every creature."

Since the beginning of this program, over 7,500 young people have ministered in 37 foreign countries. Tens of thousands more have done the same at selected sites in the United States. Youth Department statistics indicate that over 80,000 people have come to Christ as a direct result of the AIM program.

Light-for-the-Lost (a 30-year-old program of the Men's Ministries Department) supplies hundreds of thousands of pieces of literature that are distributed through AIM.

Besides assisting the denomination's outreach, the AIM program has helped young people understand evangelism. A high percentage of them later enter full-time ministry.

Mobilization and Placement Service

Mobilization and Placement Service (MAPS) is a program designed to "match people with needs." It gives support to home and foreign missions by making short-term assignments to people who have special skills and training.

Many MAPS workers are young people. High school graduates are eligible for assignment. (On the other hand, an impressive number of retired people find fulfillment in MAPS.) Those who serve must be dedicated to Christ and faithful to their local churches. Willingness, adaptability, and concern are other helpful attributes.

MAPS sponsors a variety of programs through which people can use their skills in Christian service. Summer workers and college interns are assigned to 8 weeks of ministry in construction, evangelism, office work, and local church endeavors around the world. Several hundred take part every year.

Short-term appointments allow hundreds more to serve. A large percentage of those who accept 1- and 2-year assignments are young people. Volunteers use their special skills—as accountants, carpenters, librarians, nurses, printers, teachers—to help outreaches around the world.

Construction teams, usually workers from a specific church or area, go to home and foreign missions stations to build churches and other facilities.

MAPS also offers Vocational Christian Service to guide those looking for jobs that will allow them to witness in countries not always open to missionaries. This service also supplies information for those seeking secular employment in places in this country where they can help start new Assemblies of God churches.

Other Youth Programs

Among other programs coordinated outside the Youth Department are Royal Rangers, an outreach of Men's Ministries, and Missionettes, sponsored by Women's Ministries.

At the end of World War II, the idea of forming a group of Assemblies of God men committed to witnessing and stewardship stirred up interest. The 1951 General Council authorized a Men's Fellowship Department (now Men's Ministries). After a slow start, Men's Ministries began to grow. Currently, over 4,500 churches have organized Men's Ministries groups.

Among the reasons for developing a national men's fellowship was the need for developing a training program for boys. In 1955, a program called Christian Cadets was started. It included boys and girls, but soon conflicted with the girls' outreach sponsored by Women's Ministries.

In 1962, department leaders began a new program limited to boys: Royal Rangers. Its training promotes commitment to Christ, the local church, and the community. This program has proved an effective outreach. Royal Rangers groups have been organized in 42 foreign countries, where the program has been valuable in discipling boys for Christ.

Missionettes, under the Women's Ministries Department, has proven equally effective in challenging girls to Christian witness and service. The effort to organize Assemblies of God women began in Texas in 1925. Led by Etta Calhoun, it quickly spread to other churches and districts. Finally, in 1951, the General Council authorized a national office. By then, 27 districts had their own organizations. Four years later, every district had a Women's Missionary Council (as Women's Ministries was then known).

Women's Ministries today is a cooperative fellowship of women offering opportunities for service, outreach, and personal growth. Their ministry covers five broad areas: local church and community, district, home missions, foreign missions, and benevolences. It has several auxiliaries that motivate and train young people: Rainbows (for preschoolers), Missionettes, and Ys (Young Women's Auxiliary).

By stimulating interest in missions and outreach, these programs have attracted young women to special projects and given them incentive for involvement in other programs, like AIM. The Missionettes program, begun in 1956, involves over 122,000 girls from kindergarten through junior high school in more than 16,000 registered clubs worldwide. More than 17,000 Ys meet in over 1,800 groups.

Sunday schools and the related Boys and Girls Missionary Crusade (BGMC) program have also involved youth in training and outreach. During the 1930s, after some early hesitation about regular Christian education in the church, the value of the Sunday school to the local church was recognized. It offered opportunities to disciple believers and to evangelize the unchurched. By the late 1930s, one thousand new Sunday schools were being organized annually.

During the 1940s and early 1950s, large Sunday school conventions were highlights of the denomination's history. In the 1950s, Gospel Publishing House began producing graded curriculum, offering specialized materials for ministering to Assemblies of God young people through the Sunday school.

BGMC is an effort of the Sunday School Department to raise money for Sunday school materials and training literature for the mission fields. This program appeals to children as young as 4 years old, involving them in world outreach ministries and helping them develop the habit of giving.

Probably the most well known Assemblies of God youth outreach is Teen Challenge, under the direction of the Division of Home Missions. Teen Challenge has as its basic goal "communicating the power of the gospel of Jesus Christ to troubled youth wherever they are."

To do this, Teen Challenge once held large street rallies, sometimes attracting several thousand listeners. More recently it has stressed one-to-one street ministry. Its workers go wherever there are young people in need.

Coffeehouses and "drop-in" centers are places for contact with "troubled youth." Teen Challenge representatives present programs in schools, clubs, and other public gatherings to make people aware of the program. They hold services in prisons and juvenile centers. Courts and social workers as well as parents, teachers, and professional counselors refer drug-dependent young people to the program.

Those who enter Teen Challenge begin their experience in residential facilities where they stay 2 to 3 months. Their withdrawal from drugs is without medical help. They are challenged to allow faith in Christ to give them the necessary strength.

In the centers, disciplined living is emphasized along with activities like classes, work assignments, recreation, and chapel services. Those who successfully finish this part of the program may advance to one of the training centers. The training centers are dedicated to helping students become "strong, happy, successful, victorious Christians." They also offer vocational training in jobs that are necessary for the operation of the centers. The program usually lasts 8 months. Although they are urged to complete the program, students participate voluntarily and may leave at any time.

The success rate of Teen Challenge has been praised by secular authorities. The ministry has continued to expand and develop more effective methods for reaching troubled American youth.

Assemblies of God leaders and lay persons realize the importance of giving the Fellowship's young people a sense of their heritage and making opportunities for them to learn and contribute within the Movement. This helps assure that denominational purpose and priorities continue. It also brings together a large part of the constituency in cooperative efforts, far more effective than individual activity could be.

9

The Recent Past

In recent decades, the formal structure of the Assemblies of God has expanded rapidly. Committees, boards, and executive leaders have been appointed to meet the needs of the growing constituency. The advantages of setting long-term goals and evaluating progress have been recognized.

Late in the 1950s, leaders became concerned about slowing growth. Measured by new converts, churches, and ordinations, growth fell markedly in the decade after 1957. Many reasons for this have been given, but the change troubled leaders. They firmly believed the Pentecostal experience *made* witnesses. Growth suggested spiritual vitality. The Assemblies of God looked upon itself as more than an institution: Leaders tried to preserve the nature of a revival even as the revival was necessarily becoming institutionalized.

Certainly one cause of the troubling change was simply that Assemblies of God people were becoming accepted in their communities. In many places they had put behind them the "sect mentality" of the early years. But their acceptance and advancement and respectability tended to bring complacency.

This kind of pattern can be traced in the development of any revival movement, but other factors in the religious culture also brought new challenges.

During the 1950s, parish renewal movements across the nation strengthened the religious identity of Spirit-baptized people who might have otherwise become Assemblies of God. In addition, neo-Pentecostal leaders encouraged those who sought renewal in an experience with the Holy Spirit to stay in their churches. This alternative, unavailable to most earlier Pentecostal converts, included a challenge to penetrate the denominations with the full gospel. Leaving one's church to join the classical Pentecostals was an abandonment of responsibility.

The new outpouring of the Holy Spirit in the mainstream liberal denominations had made some classical Pentecostals question the "puritanical" life-style their fellowships had historically stood for. The Assemblies of God was affected in many ways by these changes in the culture and the religious community. To some degree, it shared with other conservative evangelical groups the problems of responding to modern times.

In this climate of social and religious change, the Assemblies of God began to redefine its goals as a fellowship. A primary concern was evangelism. "Every regenerated generation must receive the Holy Spirit," they agreed. "You cannot teach people to be witnesses; they become witnesses when they have an experience of something. . . . A good Pentecostal witness is one who can tell how he got saved and healed and baptized in the Holy Spirit."

Assemblies of God leaders understood that only renewal in the local churches would cause members to "become" Pentecostal witnesses. The 1963 General Council acted to support local churches in their quest for revival and outreach. It placed the coordination of evangelism under the office of the general superintendent. One result was the creation of the Spiritual Life–

Evangelism Commission. Through it, headquarters personnel planned ways to help churches in evangelistic outreaches. They also set specific goals of growth. Underlying the plans, however, was the realization that only a "new Pentecost" could give the necessary drive.

As another part of the renewal process, the Executive Presbytery launched a self-study of the Assemblies of God. Out of this a statement of purpose was drawn up; it was explained and developed in the St. Louis Council on Evangelism in 1968.

The statement described a threefold purpose for the Assemblies of God. The Fellowship was "an agency of God for evangelizing the world; a corporate body in which man may worship God; a channel of God's purpose to build a body of saints being perfected in the image of His Son."

A Five-Year Plan of Advance gave the denomination specific goals. It symbolized the executive leaders' recognition of the relationship between evaluating goals and continuing the vitality of the Movement. Heartfelt yearning for revival stirred leaders to pray and prepare. At about the same time, the headquarters structure was reorganized to prevent the duplication of efforts and make new programs more efficient.

Separation and Social Concern

During the 1960s, the radical turn in American attitudes toward religion and morality touched the Assemblies of God as well as other denominations. In 1963, the Supreme Court ruled that religious ceremonies in public schools were unconstitutional. Throughout the decade, the civil rights movement called for social justice. The stepping up of the Viet Nam War had a hand in growing social disunity. In many places, the religious revival of the postwar years gave way to uncertainty. To many minds, America had clearly entered a "post-Christian" era.

In theology, radical thinkers talked about the "death of God" and the "secularization" of the gospel. A generation of young evangelicals on the nation's campuses were influenced by the uncertainties surrounding them. Some of them began to criticize their denominations' lack of social concern.

At the same time, it became apparent that all conservative evangelicals were no longer fully committed to the fundamentalist doctrine of the inerrancy of Scripture. In 1976, Harold Lindsell's book *The Battle for the Bible* documented the "limited inerrancy" teaching common at some leading evangelical schools. The Assemblies of God, as part of the evangelical community, shared widespread concern over changing doctrinal and cultural standards.

Evangelicals began to enjoy "intellectual sophistication," and Assemblies of God believers, like other evangelicals, became (as Richard Quebedeaux noted in *The Worldly Evangelicals*) "harder and harder to distinguish from other people."

Since its organization in 1914, the Assemblies of God had firmly declared the need for separation from the world. In 1914, Pentecostals generally agreed with other fundamentalist evangelicals about what *separation* meant: modesty in dress and appearance, as well as abstinence from alcohol, smoking, gambling, dancing, theater attendance, and other such amusements.

Those with backgrounds in the holiness movements often lengthened the list of unacceptable practices. In effect, some made certain norms of dress, diet, and behavior a basic part of the Christian life-style. Many forbade the eating of pork and/or the drinking of coffee, tea, or Coca-Cola. Some objected to the wearing of any jewelry or ornamentation or ties, refusing to wear even wedding rings. Among some groups, objections to spectator sports included the things associated with them—like bubble gum and Cracker Jacks.

Among the early members of the Assemblies of God were also many who had been deeply influenced by the ministries of A. B. Simpson, R. A. Torrey, and other premillennialists who stressed the person and work of the Holy Spirit. In this evangelical setting, a cause-and-effect relationship between conduct and "communion" with the Holy Spirit was taught.

"How carefully we ought to walk in all things," Torrey wrote, "so as not to grieve Him who dwells within us." Fellowship with the Holy Spirit "cost" the believer "absolute obedience," Simpson cautioned. "Don't disobey Him; if you do, you will lose something."

Moody advised believers to test their conduct by its effect on their "communion" with the Holy Spirit. "Why do . . . Christians go after . . . worldly amusements?" Torrey asked. "Either because they have never definitely received the Holy Spirit, or else because the fountain is choked."

Such teaching flourished in the settings from which many early Pentecostals came. It tried to force conscious choices between the Holy Spirit and the spirit of the age. While some matters were left to individual conscience, there was a general agreement about acceptable and unacceptable behavior.

As time passed, however, and cultural standards changed, a new generation in the Assemblies of God questioned what they saw as "legalism" in the older generation. Although a range of "acceptable" behavior (depending to some degree on geographic location) still exists,

Assemblies of God people are less outwardly conspicuous in society than they once were.

The leadership has consistently called the Fellowship to a life-style of holiness and separation. In the last 15 years, it has also begun to develop official positions on some issues of general concern. Since 1970, the General Presbytery has adopted a series of position papers defining a Biblical perspective on matters within both the evangelical community and the wider culture.

The first paper, put out in 1970, explained the denomination's views on the inerrancy of Scripture. Several other doctrines have since been similarly clarified. Issues raised by the charismatic movement were addressed in other statements. More recently, the General Presbytery has adopted reports relating to homosexuality and gambling. Committees are currently preparing statements on drinking and abortion.

As homosexuality, gambling, drinking, and abortion have emerged as major cultural concerns, some within the Assemblies of God have become active in nonevangelistic efforts to address them. Within the denomination, promotion of an awareness of social duty has brought about some members' participation in efforts to change things in society at large.

Although American Pentecostal priorities have usually placed evangelism before social concern, the Assemblies of God has shown interest in meeting welfare needs within the constituency. Many congregations also offer practical help in times of community need.

A program providing for aged ministers was begun in 1933. Administered through the Division of the Treasury, it has given assistance to over 1,000 retired ministers.

The Fellowship also keeps an emergency fund for helping churches in times of disaster. The Benevolences Department oversees Hillcrest Children's Home, opened in 1944, and Highlands Child Placement Service, an agency in Kansas City that includes a program for unmarried mothers as well as adoption services. In May 1972, a nursing care/retirement complex, Maranatha Village, was begun and now accommodates over 400 residents.

Through efforts like these, the Fellowship seeks to care for its members and to offer services to others in need.

The Role of Women

The American Pentecostal movement has displayed a variety of attitudes toward the role of women in ministry. Many women played a large part in the early Pentecostal revival. Some of them gained wide reputations as preachers and writers.

In the Assemblies of God, Carrie Judd Montgomery pastored a church in California, surpervised a faith home, and edited a paper called *Triumphs of Faith.* Lilian Yeomans taught, preached, and wrote, emphasizing divine healing. Alice Reynolds Flower wrote Sunday school literature as well as other material for publication in the Fellowship's periodicals. Marie Burgess Brown founded a Pentecostal mission in New York City in 1907. It became Glad Tidings Tabernacle, and she served as assistant pastor and pastor for a total of 64 years. Many women dedicated their lives to foreign missions.

Notable women in the early history of the Assemblies of God had received training—and sometimes ordination—in their pre-Pentecostal days. In the nondenominational settings that stressed the ministry of the Holy Spirit, women were allowed relative freedom to participate publicly. At the turn of the century, those seeking revival around the country often stressed Peter's words at the Jerusalem Pentecost: "Your sons *and your daughters* shall prophesy."

As A. J. Gordon pointed out in the late 19th century: "In order to have a right understanding of this subject, it is necessary for us to be reminded that we are living in the dispensation of the Spirit. . . . [This] prophecy of Joel, realized at Pentecost . . . gives to woman a status in the Spirit hitherto unknown. . . . Here is woman's equal warrant with man's for telling out the gospel of the grace of God."

By the time the Assemblies of God organized, many of the Christian groups from which most of its first members came generally conceded that women could give public utterances, exercise spiritual gifts, pray publicly, teach, and engage in missionary work. On the other hand, women were generally discouraged from taking administrative leadership. Married women in public ministries—like those who were not—were expected to show "loving loyalty" to their husbands.

In the early Pentecostal movement, having the "anointing" was far more important than one's sex. As evangelistic bands carried the full gospel across the country, women who were recognized as having the anointing of the Holy Spirit shared with men in the preaching ministry.

Those women who took part in the early development of the Assemblies of God seem to have given relatively little consideration to their "rights" of ministry. Rather, they believed that if God gave someone a ministry, He would also give the opportunity to carry it out. A person's call—and how other believers viewed it—was more important than "papers" (that is, formal denominational licensing).

We have already noted that some women had been ordained or licensed for ministry before coming into the

Assemblies of God. The organization accepted their credentials, but recommended that women be ordained only as evangelists and missionaries. It withheld from them the right to serve as "elders" (a term often used synonymously with "pastors").

This formal position was actually more liberal than that of several other Pentecostal denominations. In most such groups, women played a vital role in pioneer efforts, but sometimes found themselves restricted in decision-making roles to prayerful support for the men.

In 1920 women received the right to speak and vote at General Councils, the same year they could vote for the first time in a national presidential election. During the 1920s, reports mentioned the role of women in the Movement's growth, pointing to "God's hand upon many women to proclaim and publish the 'good tidings of great joy' in a wonderful way."

Through 1933, each General Council had repeated itself on the right of women to be ordained as evangelists and missionaries and encouraged them to serve as assistant pastors. Then in 1935, the Council reversed its policy of refusing to credential women pastors and declared that the ordination of women "to the ministry of the gospel" enabled them to serve "either as evangelists or as pastors as their qualifications warrant." "The right to administer the ordinances of the church, when such acts are necessary," the provision read, "shall be included in the ordination." Women seeking such ordination had to be at least 25 years old, with a "generally accepted ministry" and "qualifications proved in actual service."

Since 1935, the Assemblies of God has ordained both women and men to the various types of ministry sponsored by the Fellowship. Officially, then, the denomination maintains that God gives "ministry gifts" to women. In holding this position, the Assemblies of God has offered opportunities to women that few other organized Pentecostal groups have equaled.

However, the percentage of Assemblies of God women pastors has always been small. Widely held American assumptions about a woman's place in the church are evident in Pentecostalism. This is because Pentecostal people have come to identify with middle-class America.

But the Fellowship's history shows that when sensitivity to the Spirit predominates, the question of "feminist" rights is less relevant than that of anointing and calling. An early issue of the *Apostolic Faith* expressed the ideal. The believer's sex didn't matter, but availability did. "Whenever the Lord wants to play His piano," Pentecostals were told, "He tunes up the harp and plays with His own fingers." Men and women were simply to be available for divine use.

The classical Pentecostal position holds that both men and women should be at all times fully open to the leading of the Spirit. Believers share a responsibility to allow one another to function at all times "in the Spirit."

Marriage and the Family

On the other hand, Assemblies of God leaders have recognized that a balanced view is essential. In response to recent social changes in the family, the Assemblies of God has begun to focus on family life.

Through marriage enrichment seminars, Fellowship leaders have offered Biblical teaching to strengthen the marriage relationship. Many within the Fellowship have historically opposed divorce and remarriage. Recent trends have raised disturbing issues.

Questions about ministers who had been divorced and remarried were brought before Assemblies of God leaders shortly after they organized in 1914. They decided not to offer credentials to ministers who had been divorced and remarried or who had spouses who had been.

By the early 1920s, the denomination discouraged pastors from performing marriage ceremonies in which one partner was divorced from a companion who was still living. Throughout the years, the policy on this issue has often been brought up.

In the 1970s, the rising number of divorces in American society and the marital complications new converts brought with them into the Assemblies of God called for a fresh, detailed consideration of the subject. A report presented to the 1973 General Council cleared up ambiguities in the earlier position and called for limited change. While continuing to maintain that "God hates divorce," the Council voted to permit ministers, using certain guidelines, to perform marriage ceremonies for people who had been divorced. It refused to change its ruling to withhold credentials from ministers who had been divorced or had married a partner who had been divorced.

Recent cultural trends, including the decision of more young people to remain single and the need of many married women to work, have resulted in the Assemblies of God's development of programs to address the spiritual and social needs of new categories of adults.

Assemblies of God attitudes toward family life are part of broader conditions in which acceptable roles for women are defined. Changing patterns of family relationships have raised new issues for the Movement in the same way that institutionalization and social mobility did. Increased absorption of the culture by much of the Assemblies of God constituency has brought the problems of American society into the denomination with new force.

The denomination has been generally negative toward contemporary feminism, reaffirming a rejection of related issues, such as abortion and sexual permissiveness. But issues raised by the secular culture have again set in motion efforts to find Biblical viewpoints on the present place of women in the church, relationships in the home, and the believer's obligations toward society. These issues have combined with other factors to encourage family-oriented programs and activities in the Assemblies of God. The consensus seems to be that the best way to meet contemporary cultural pressures is (1) to pray for a revival of holiness and (2) to offer believers incentives to explore the potential and obligations of Christian family relationships.

The Charismatic Renewal

During the 1970s, the leadership's prayers and efforts for renewal found response among the constituency. Throughout the Fellowship, an emphasis on prayer and on the Holy Spirit accompanied the quest for revival. By the end of the decade, the Assemblies of God had become one of the fastest-growing denominations in the United States.

In an article in the *Saturday Evening Post* in the summer of 1982, journalist Edward Plowman described the character of the contemporary Assemblies of God. He found three "dominant religious characteristics": "love for God," "intense desire that others might come to know and love Him, too," and "rock-ribbed belief in the authority of the Bible." Plowman noted also the wide range of worship styles, due partly to pastoral preference and partly to congregational tradition.

Assemblies of God churches reflect the culture of the communities they serve. Ethnic outreaches flourish in America's cities, where a growing number of congregations minister to inner-city needs. After several decades during which middle-class congregations moved to suburbia, new efforts to evangelize urban America have been launched through the appropriate districts, and older congregations have seen renewal.

In the last decade, Assemblies of God churches have continued to reach out to America's unchurched. They have also attracted followers from the charismatic movement.

Charismatic believers have turned to the Assemblies of God for nurture and stability. In turn, they have contributed to local Assemblies of God congregations in at least two ways: (1) by bringing a fresh awareness of the vital presence and transforming power of the Holy Spirit (often resulting in greater spontaneity and openness to the Holy Spirit in the churches) and (2) by strengthening the middle-class identity of the growing denomination.

Pentecostalism was once dismissed as the religion of America's dispossessed. Before the charismatic movement, that image had begun to change. By the 1970s, Pentecostalism had gained respect among the middle class. Among Pentecostals a growing number of professionals were found. At the same time, the Movement also showed a new awareness of an obligation to the dispossessed. This found expression in new urban efforts.

In Summary

For the past 25 years, General Superintendent Zimmerman has guided the Assemblies of God. Under his leadership the denomination has experienced remarkable growth. Its earlier moves toward broader evangelical and Pentecostal association have become firm commitments.

Since 1967, Zimmerman has been on the Board of Managers of the American Bible Society. In 1974, he became part of the newly formed Lausanne Committee for World Evangelization. In 1983, his religious statesmanship was recognized in his appointment as Protestant vice-chairman for the Year of the Bible.

Zimmerman's spirituality, integrity, and executive ability have helped gain respect for the Assemblies of God in the broader American religious community. He has also led the Assemblies of God into a closer relationship with fellow Pentecostals around the world.

His view of the Assemblies of God as part of an ongoing revival has made him favor growth and change. He has accepted the challenge of achieving Pentecostalism's potential in the broader contemporary religious context. At the same time, he has worked to keep the "old landmarks" of the denomination's heritage.

The balance the executives and presbyters of the Assemblies of God try to strike is critical to the Movement's future. A loosely structured, cooperative fellowship has become a denomination; yet it maintains qualities of a revival movement open to the workings of the Holy Spirit. But the effects of several generations of members being born into the denomination have had to be taken into account. For example, some are Pentecostals in name only, never having experienced the baptism in the Holy Spirit. As national and local leaders plan evangelistic outreaches, they recognize the constant need for renewal within the Assemblies of God.

Through their association with the Assemblies of God, local churches attest to the rich, diverse heritage of the 20th-century Pentecostal revival. That heritage brings them both identity and responsibility. It offers direction to a generation of Pentecostals who are a recognized part of a broader evangelical culture. And it helps the Fellowship preserve its uniqueness in that culture.

History is important. To understand the Fellowship's present situation and its future potential, a person must explore its past: identifying where it came from, examining its social setting, tracing its development. Individuals, churches, districts, and national leaders need to continually relate to their Pentecostal heritage. This will keep before them the importance of the Movement's reliance on the Holy Spirit. Each issue of the *Pentecostal Evangel* carries the words that have become, in a sense, the motto of the Assemblies of God: "Not by might, nor by power, but by My Spirit, saith the Lord."

Like those who established their roots more than 80 years ago, today's Pentecostals sing of what refreshes their personal experience and motivates their evangelistic outreach:

> Oh, spread the tidings round
> Wherever man is found,
> Wherever human hearts
> And human woes abound;
> Let every Christian tongue
> Proclaim the joyful sound:
> The Comforter has come.

Each generation must both experience its own Pentecostal revival and learn the discipline of the Spirit-filled life if the movement called the Assemblies of God is to retain its force and achieve its potential, under God, throughout the world.

Left, Charles Fox Parham, who called himself "progenitor" of the Apostolic Faith Movement. Right, Marie Burgess Brown, who brought the Pentecostal message to New York City in 1907. She and her husband, Robert, pastored Glad Tidings Tabernacle for many years.

Burgess' storefront mission was typical of many early Pentecostal meeting places.

Azusa Street Mission, Los Angeles, where the Pentecostal revival centered for several years (from 1906).

Some early Pentecostal leaders: W. J. Seymour (front left), who led the Azusa St. Mission, John Lake (beside Seymour), and F. F. Bosworth (standing, center).

RED-HOT STUFF

WHAT RIGHT HAVE THESE BUZZARDS AND BUZZERS
TO COME INTO OUR MIDST AND TRY TO SUPPLANT
THE PRINCIPLES OF OUR COMMUNITY LIFE, AND FEED
UPON THE CARRION WHICH HAS FALLEN IN OUR MIDST?

LET THESE HAWKS TAKE THEIR CARRION.
FLY AWAY. AND BUILD A CITY OF THEIR OWN!

THEY HAVE NO RIGHT TO INTERFERE OR MEDDLE WITH
OUR INSTITUTIONAL LIFE, AND IF THEY WERE HONEST
THEY WOULD LEAVE THIS WORK WITH THOSE WHO HELPED
TO BUILD IT, AND LET THEM SOLVE THE PROBLEMS
UPON THE BASIS OF ZION'S FUNDAMENTAL PRINCIPLES—
THE PRINCIPLES WHICH BROUGHT ZION PEOPLE TOGETHER

JUST TAKE A GOOD LOOK AT THIS ARMY OF
EFFEMINATE LEADERS—PARHAM, OLD TOM, LAKE
FOCKLER, SPEICHER! WHAT A QUINTETTE OF PURITY

—— PROFESSOR BENJAMIN G. HESS, AUTHOR.

Anti-Pentecostal expressions were frequent. This was posted in Zion City, Illinois.

Members of the first Executive Presbytery of the Assemblies of God. Left to right, row 1: T. K. Leonard, E. N. Bell, Cyrus Fockler. Row 2: J. W. Welch, J. R. Flower, D. C. Opperman, Howard Goss, M. M. Pinson.

Early editorial offices, Gospel Publishing House. Left to right: Alice Frodsham, Stanley Frodsham, Charles Robinson.

A gospel car, used for evangelism during the 1920s by Ernest S. Williams and his Philadelphia congregation. Williams is the second from the left.

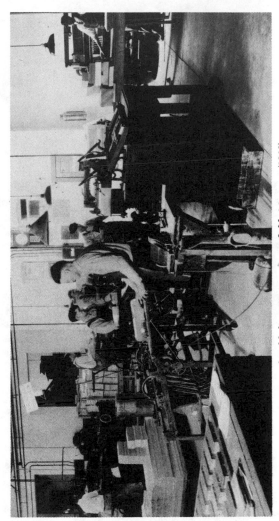

Gospel Publishing House, Springfield, Missouri (1928).

Central Assembly, Springfield, Missouri, the first location of Central Bible Institute (1922).

Left, Daniel and Mattie Kerr, leaders in the formulation of doctrine and the establishing of Bible schools. Right, Noel Perkin (right) and J. R. Flower (left) visit the A. E. Wilsons, missionaries in Upper Volta (1937).

Ambassador II, one of two planes purchased by Speed-the-Light to ease missionary travel during the late 1940s.

Missionary Florence Steidel welcoming Liberian President William Tubman (1944-1971) to her mission station.

Left, Mark Buntain, missionary to India, with one of the many children to whom he has ministered. Right, Fred Vogler, the first national home missions executive.

Wesley R. Steelberg, *Revivaltime* speaker and general superintendent (1949-1952).

Executives read the Springfield newspaper lead story about the transfer of the Army's O'Reilly Hospital building to the Assemblies of God. It became Evangel College. Seated, General Supt. Ralph Riggs; standing, left to right, J. R. Flower, Bert Webb, J. R. Ashcroft, Gayle Lewis, Thomas F. Zimmerman.

Alice Reynolds Flower, holding copies of the *Christian Evangel*, the paper she and her husband began in 1913, and a recent *Pentecostal Evangel*.

Main entrance to headquarters complex, Springfield, Missouri.

Left, David Wilkerson preaching at a street meeting. Wilkerson founded Teen Challenge. Right, Thomas F. Zimmerman, general superintendent since 1959.

Glossary

apostolic faith. The term American Pentecostals first used to
describe themselves. They believed their movement was a
last-days restoration of Christianity to how it was practiced
by the apostles in New Testament times. Associates of Charles
Parham used the term to identify their missions and camp
meetings. After 1909, many began to use the term *Pentecostal* instead. Some Pentecostal groups, however, still use
the term *apostolic faith*.

Assemblies of God. The common designation of local churches
affiliated with The General Council of the Assemblies of God.

charismatic movement. Broadly defined, any religious movement emphasizing the gifts of the Holy Spirit (called *char-
ismata* in the Greek language of the New Testament). More
specifically, since the 1950s, the movement penetrating non-
Pentecostal (and usually old-line) denominations that has
promoted the presence of the Spirit and His gifts.

classical Pentecostals. Members of denominations or congregations that trace their Pentecostal roots directly or indirectly
to the ministry of Charles Parham (1901-1909). The largest
such American denominations are the Assemblies of God,
the Church of God in Christ, and the Church of God (Cleveland, Tennessee).

denominationalism. Narrowly defined, it is a negative view of
churches organizing into a denomination. Pentecostals tended
to look upon all church denominations as enemies and tried
to avoid their centralization of authority and formalization of
worship. This attitude was expressed by William Durham
when he claimed that denominationalizing trends had killed
every major revival in church history. Such antidenomina-

tionalism led some Pentecostals to dismiss other Protestants as members of "denominational churches"; the phrase had negative overtones. Some Pentecostals continue to reject the term *denomination* even after their own fellowships have become full-fledged denominations.

dispensationalism. The dividing of history into specific periods according to how God is said to have dealt with humanity. For example, from the Fall to Noah, God related to man through his conscience, from Moses to Christ, He related to man through the Law, and so forth. Late 19th-century premillennialists held that God had a "pattern for the ages." Composed of seven dispensations, the last would be the Millennium. Dispensationalism was made popular through the notes of the *Scofield Reference Bible*. It came to be more than a way of looking at history; it was tied to the verbal inerrancy of the Bible.

Executive Presbytery. The trustees of The General Council of the Assemblies of God. These men, representing different regions of the nation, oversee all departments of the denomination, arrange for the biennial General Councils, and act for the corporation between General Council sessions. This group was part of the original structure of The General Council of the Assemblies of God.

"faith" efforts. Early Pentecostals used the adjective *faith* to mean "without visible means of support." They trusted God to supply all the needs of their *faith* efforts and considered it improper to ask for funds or to publicize needs. With this understanding of the word, they went out as faith missionaries, without boards or pledged support; opened faith missions across the country; ran faith Bible schools and faith homes; and lived faith lives. Parham's followers considered this position essential to true Pentecostal ministry.

finished work of Calvary. The view of sanctification developed by William Durham, A. S. Copley, and others who claimed that the believer was sanctified by identification with Christ in His death and resurrection. Sanctification was a process that continued until death. This contrasted with the way most early Pentecostals understood sanctification: They thought it was a definite one-time experience that followed conversion.

fundamentalism. Generally speaking, a group that formed within evangelicalism by the end of the 19th century. Its followers held that Scripture was inspired word for word and had the final say in everything. This position became central to their theology. Many of them were dispensationalists or pre-millennialists, or both. The name *fundamentalism* came to be linked with a series of booklets titled "The Fundamentals," which had been edited by some of the leaders of fundamentalism. In this connection, fundamentalism also came to suggest several specific explanations of fundamentals of the faith, such as the Virgin Birth, the substitutionary Atonement, and the physical Resurrection.

After World War I, fundamentalists became more and more exclusive and defensive, bickering among themselves and attacking those conservative evangelicals who had anything to do with Christians who were not fundamentalists.

General Council. Assemblies of God ministers and church representatives in biennial session.

The General Council of the Assemblies of God. Legal corporation title.

General Presbytery. Representative body that advises the Executive Presbytery, sets policy between General Council sessions, and serves as a court of appeal in matters of ministerial discipline. Instituted at the 1916 General Council.

holiness movement. A broad movement in 19th-century American religion, related but not confined to the family of Methodist denominations. Participants stressed sanctification as a definite second experience for every Christian. They were concerned about personal perfection, and many emphasized the Holy Spirit. Some made important contributions to efforts to perfect American society.

"latter rain." With reference to prophecies in Joel 2:23 and Zechariah 10:1, early Pentecostals used the term *latter rain* to describe the 20th-century outpouring of the Holy Spirit. The term also came to have dispensational overtones as Bible teachers like D. Wesley Myland considered the details of God's dealings with His people in the last days. Focus on the Pentecostal revival as the prophesied "latter rain" reinforced the strong stress on the soon return of Christ. (See *new order of the latter rain.*)

neoevangelicalism (or new evangelicalism). Those evangelicals who, since World War II, have tried to stress the positive proclamation of their message, to identify readily with others who share their faith, to develop an integrated theology, to face honestly the challenges of science and philosophy and the ambiguities in their own heritage, to emphasize education, and to express social concerns. This is in contrast to the fundamentalism of the 1920s and 1930s, which was often defensive, negative, divisive, and opposed to learning about anything but the Bible.

new issue. The doctrine, which gained acceptance among Pentecostals after 1913, that Jesus is the Old Testament Jehovah and that baptism "in the name of Jesus" is necessary for the forgiveness of sins. Also known as "oneness" and "Jesus only" because of its teaching that Jesus is the only Person in the Godhead and that Jesus is "the name" of the Father, Son, and Holy Spirit. Its advocates based much of their practical message on Acts 2:38.

new order of the "latter rain." A movement within Pentecostalism during the late 1940s and early 1950s that stressed prophecy, laying on of hands to impart spiritual gifts, and organizing churches around prophets and apostles. Participants opposed denominational organization and denounced the Pentecostal fellowships as "dead." They felt their movement was a greater outpouring of the prophesied "latter rain" than the early Pentecostal revival had been.

premillennialism. The view that Christ's second coming will happen before the 1,000 years of righteousness known as the Millennium. Pentecostals generally believe the Second Coming includes the secret rapture of the Church just before 7 years of tribulation. These years will be followed by Christ's return with His saints to rule on earth for 1,000 years. The expectation of Christ's "any moment" coming served as an incentive to holiness and evangelism.

restorationism. The effort to bring back early Christian practices. In some cases, this includes restoration of church offices and how the church ought to govern itself as well as restoration of doctrine and experience. Restorationists tend to ignore historical development and to base their teaching directly on the New Testament. Some early Pentecostals expected restoration of the power of New Testament Christianity just before Jesus' return. They accepted the baptism

157

in the Holy Spirit as part of a larger recreation of the vitality of the Early Church.

sanctification. Suggests both separation from evil and dedication to God. The Assemblies of God holds that sanctification "is realized" when the believer identifies with Christ's death and resurrection. It is maintained by "reckoning daily on the fact of that union" and by "offering every faculty continually to the dominion of the Holy Spirit." This view is often spoken of as *progressive* sanctification. (See also *finished work of Calvary.*)

second definite work of grace. A phrase describing sanctification, used by those who believe that sanctification is a sudden, definite experience that follows conversion.

uniform initial evidence. The teaching that speaking in tongues is always the evidence of the baptism in the Holy Spirit. The Assemblies of God teaches that speaking in tongues is the initial physical evidence of Spirit baptism. The denomination has tried to discourage seekers from preoccupation with speaking in tongues. Although tongues is the accepted evidence of a vital experience, other traits should be evident in Spirit-filled believers. These include "an overflowing fullness of the Spirit"; "a deepened reverence for God"; "intensified consecration to God and dedication to his work"; "a more active love for Christ, for His Word, and for the lost."

Wesleyan. Belonging to the teaching of John Wesley (1703-1791) or the groups that grew out of his ministry. Wesley, an ordained Anglican priest, devoted his life to evangelism. In his words, he sought "to promote as far as I am able vital practical religion and by the grace of God to beget, preserve, and increase the life of God in the souls of men." He stressed the need for "inward" and "outward" holiness as well as religious experience. His message of free, available grace was a central part of the extensive 18th-century evangelical revival. Ably assisted by his brother Charles and George Whitefield, John Wesley was the central figure in the rise of Methodism.

Index